Doggin' The Tidewater

The 33 Best Places To Hike With Your Dog From The Northern Neck To Virginia Beach

DOUG GELBERT

illustrations by

ANDREW CHESWORTH

Cruden Bay Books

There is always a new trail to look forward to...

DOGGIN' THE TIDEWATER: THE 33 BEST PLACES
TO HIKE WITH YOUR DOG FROM THE
NORTHERN NECK TO VIRIGNIA BEACH

Cruden Bay Books
PO Box 467
Montchanin, DE 19710
www.hikewithyourdog.com

International Standard Book Number 978-0-9797074-0-7

*"Dogs are our link to paradise...to sit with a dog on a hillside
on a glorious afternoon is to be back in Eden,
where doing nothing was not boring - it was peace."*
- Milan Kundera

Ahead On The Trail

Introduction

The Tidewater can be a great place to hike with your dog. Paw-friendly sand trails, shady maritime forests, some of the most historic grounds in America, the estates of Virginia's wealthiest families and some of the country's dog-friendliest beaches all beckon to your canine adventurer.

I have selected what I consider to be the 33 best places to take your dog for an outing in the Tidewater and ranked them according to subjective criteria including the variety of hikes available, opportunities for canine swimming and pleasure of the walks. The rankings include a mix of parks that feature long walks and parks that contain short walks. Did I miss your favorite? Let us know at *www.hikewithyourdog.com*.

For dog owners it is important to realize that not all parks are open to our best trail companions (see page 14 for a list of parks that do not allow dogs). It is sometimes hard to believe but not everyone loves dogs. We are, in fact, in the minority when compared with our non-dog owning neighbors.

So when visiting a park always keep your dog under control and clean up any messes and we can all expect our great parks to remain open to our dogs. And maybe some others will see the light as well. *Remember, every time you go out with your dog you are an ambassador for all dog owners.*

Grab that leash and hit the trail!
DBG

Hiking With Your Dog

So you want to start hiking with your dog. Hiking with your dog can be a fascinating way to explore the Tidewater from a canine perspective. Some things to consider:

🐾 Dog's Health

Hiking can be a wonderful preventative for any number of physical and behavioral disorders. One in every three dogs is overweight and running up trails and leaping through streams is great exercise to help keep pounds off. Hiking can also relieve boredom in a dog's routine and calm dogs prone to destructive habits. And hiking with your dog strengthens the overall owner/dog bond.

🐾 Breed of Dog

All dogs enjoy the new scents and sights of a trail. But some dogs are better suited to hiking than others. If you don't as yet have a hiking companion, select a breed that matches your interests. Do you look forward to an entire afternoon's hiking? You'll need a dog bred to keep up with such a pace, such as a retriever or a spaniel. Is a half-hour enough walking for you? It may not be for an energetic dog like a border collie. If you already have a hiking friend, tailor your plans to his abilities.

🐾 Conditioning

Just like humans, dogs need to be acclimated to the task at hand. An inactive dog cannot be expected to bounce from the easy chair in the den to complete a 3-hour hike. You must also be physically able to restrain your dog if confronted with distractions on the trail (like a scampering squirrel or a pack of joggers). Have your dog checked by a veterinarian before significantly increasing his activity level.

🐾 Weather

Hot humid summers do not do dogs any favors. With no sweat glands and only panting available to disperse body heat, dogs are much more susceptible to heat stroke than we are. Unusually rapid panting and/or a bright red tongue are signs of heat exhaustion in your pet.

Always carry enough water for your hike. Even days that don't seem too warm can cause discomfort in dark-coated dogs if the sun is shining brightly. In cold weather, short-coated breeds may require additional attention.

🐾 Trail Hazards

Dogs won't get poison ivy but they can transfer it to you. Some trails are littered with small pieces of broken glass that can slice a dog's paws. Nasty thorns can also blanket trails that we in shoes may never notice. At the beach beware of sand spurs that can often be present in scrubby, sandy areas.

🐾 Ticks

You won't be able to spend much time near Tidewater swamps without encountering ticks. All are nasty but the deer tick - no bigger than a pin head - carries with it the spectre of Lyme disease. Lyme disease attacks a dog's joints and makes walking painful. The tick needs to be embedded in the skin to transmit Lyme disease. It takes 4-6 hours for a tick to become embedded and another 24-48 hours to transmit Lyme disease bacteria.

When hiking, walk in the middle of trails away from tall grass and bushes. And when the summer sun fades away don't stop thinking about ticks - they remain active any time the temperature is above 30 degrees. By checking your dog - and yourself - thoroughly after each walk you can help avoid Lyme disease. Ticks tend to congregate on your dog's ears, between the toes and around the neck and head.

🐾 Water

Surface water, including fast-flowing streams, is likely to be infested with a microscopic protozoa called *Giardia*, waiting to wreak havoc on a dog's intestinal system. The most common symptom is crippling diarrhea. Algae, pollutants and contaminants can all be in streams, ponds and puddles. If possible, carry fresh water for your dog on the trail - your dog can even learn to drink happily from a squirt bottle.

At the beach, cool sea water will be tempting for your dog but try to limit any drinking as much as possible. Again, have plenty of fresh water available for your dog to drink instead.

Rattlesnakes and Copperheads, etc.

Rattlesnakes and their close cousins, copperheads, are not particularly aggressive animals but you should treat any venomous snake with respect and keep your distance. A rattler's colors may vary but they are recognized by the namesake rattle on the tail and a diamond-shaped head. Unless cornered or teased by humans or dogs, a rattlesnake will crawl away and avoid striking. Avoid placing your hand in unexamined rocky areas and crevasses and try and keep your dog from doing so as well. If you hear a nearby rattle, stop immediately and hold your dog back. Identify where the snake is and slowly back away.

If you or your dog is bitten, do not panic but get to a hospital or veterinarian with as little physical movement as possible. Wrap between the bite and the heart. Rattlesnakes might give "dry bites" where no poison is injected, but you should always check with a doctor after a bite even if you feel fine.

Black Bears

Are you likely to see a bear while out hiking with your dog? No, it's not likely. It is, however, quite a thrill if you are fortunate enough to spot a black bear on the trail - from a distance.

Black bear attacks are incredibly rare. In the year 2000 a hiker was killed by a black bear in Great Smoky National Park and it was the first deadly bear attack in the 66-year history of America's most popular national park. It was the first EVER in the southeastern United States. In all of North America only 43 black bear mauling deaths have ever been recorded (through 1999).

Most problems with black bears occur near a campground (like the above incident) where bears have learned to forage for unprotected food. On the trail bears will typically see you and leave the area. What should you do if you encounter a black bear? Experts agree on three important things:

1) Never run. A bear will outrun you, outclimb you, outswim you. Don't look like prey.
2) Never get between a female bear and a cub who may be nearby feeding.
3) Leave a bear an escape route.

If the bear is at least 15 feet away and notices you make sure you keep your dog close and calm. If a bear stands on its hind legs or comes closer it may just be trying to get a better view or smell to evaluate the situation. Wave your arms and make noise to scare the bear away. Most bears will quickly leave the area.

If you encounter a black bear at close range, stand upright and make yourself appear as large a foe as possible. Avoid direct eye contact and speak in a calm, assertive and assuring voice as you back up slowly and out of danger.

Outfitting Your Dog For A Hike

These are the basics for taking your dog on a hike:

▶ **Collar.**
It should not be so loose as to come off but you should be able to slide your flat hand under the collar.

▶ **Identification Tags.**
Get one with your veterinarian's phone number as well.

▶ **Bandanna.**
Can help distinguish him from game in hunting season.

▶ **Leash.**
Leather lasts forever but if there's water in your dog"s future, consider quick-drying nylon.

▶ **Water.**
Carry 8 ounces for every hour of hiking.

🐾 *I want my dog to help carry water, snacks and other supplies on the trail. Where do I start?*
To select an appropriate dog pack measure your dog's girth around the rib cage. A dog pack should fit securely without hindering the dog's ability to walk normally.

🐾 *Will my dog wear a pack?*
Wearing a dog pack is no more obtrusive than wearing a collar, although some dogs will take to a pack easier than others. Introduce the pack by draping a towel over your dog's back in the house and then having your dog wear an empty pack on short walks. Progressively add some crumpled newspaper and then bits of clothing. Fill the pack with treats and reward your dog from the stash. Soon your dog will associate the dog pack with an outdoor adventure and will eagerly look forward to wearing it.

🐾 *How much weight can I put into a dog pack?*

Many dog packs are sold by weight recommendations. A healthy, well-conditioned dog can comfortably carry 25% to 33% of its body weight. Breeds prone to back problems or hip dysplasia should not wear dog packs. Consult your veterinarian before stuffing the pouches with gear.

🐾 *How does a dog wear a pack?*

The pack, typically with cargo pouches on either side, should ride as close to the shoulders as possible without limiting movement. The straps that hold the dog pack in place should be situated where they will not cause chafing.

🐾 *What are good things to put in a dog pack?*

Low density items such as food and poop bags are good choices. Ice cold bottles of water can cool your dog down on hot days. Don't put anything in a dog pack that can break. Dogs will bang the pack on rocks and trees as they wiggle through tight spots in the trail. Dogs also like to lie down in creeks and other wet spots so seal items in plastic bags. A good use for dog packs when on day hikes around the Tidewater is trail maintenance - your dog can pack out trash left by inconsiderate visitors before you.

🐾 Are dog booties a good idea?

Dog booties can be an asset, especially for the occasional canine hiker whose paw pads have not become toughened. In some places, there may be broken glass. Hiking boots for dogs are designed to prevent pads from cracking while trotting across rough surfaces. Used in winter, dog booties provide warmth and keep ice balls from forming between toe pads when hiking through snow.

🐾 What should a doggie first aid kit include?

Even when taking short hikes it is a good idea to have some basics available for emergencies:

- 4" square gauze pads
- cling type bandaging tapes
- topical wound disinfectant cream
- tweezers
- insect repellent - no reason to leave your dog unprotected against mosquitoes and yellow flies
- veterinarian's phone number

"I can't think of anything that brings me closer to tears than when my old dog - completely exhausted after a hard day in the field - limps away from her nice spot in front of the fire and comes over to where I'm sitting and puts her head in my lap, a paw over my knee, and closes her eyes, and goes back to sleep. I don't know what I've done to deserve that kind of friend."
-Gene Hill

Low Impact Hiking With Your Dog

Every time you hike with your dog on the trail you are an ambassador for all dog owners. Some people you meet won't believe in your right to take a dog on the trail. Be friendly to all and make the best impression you can by practicing low impact hiking with your dog:

- Pack out everything you pack in.

- Do not leave dog scat on the trail; if you haven't brought plastic bags for poop removal bury it away from the trail and topical water sources.

- Hike only where dogs are allowed.

- Stay on the trail.

- Do not allow your dog to chase wildlife.

- Step off the trail and wait with your dog while horses and other hikers pass.

- Do not allow your dog to bark - people are enjoying the trail for serenity.

- *Have as much fun on your hike as your dog does.*

The Other End Of The Leash

Leash laws are like speed limits - everyone seems to have a private interpretation of their validity. Some dog owners never go outside with an unleashed dog; others treat the laws as suggestions or disregard them completely. It is not the purpose of this book to tell dog owners where to go to evade the leash laws or reveal the parks where rangers will look the other way at an unleashed dog. Nor is it the business of this book to preach vigilant adherence to the leash laws. Nothing written in a book is going to change people's behavior with regard to leash laws. So this will be the last time leash laws are mentioned, save occasionally when we point out the parks where dogs are welcomed off leash.

How To Pet A Dog
Tickling tummies slowly and gently works wonders.
Never use a rubbing motion; this makes dogs bad-tempered.
A gentle tickle with the tips of the fingers is all that is necessary
to induce calm in a dog. I hate strangers who go up to dogs with their
hands held to the dog's nose, usually palm towards themselves.
How does the dog know that the hand doesn't hold something horrid?
The palm should always be shown to the dog and go straight
down to between the dog's front legs and tickle gently with
a soothing voice to accompany the action.
Very often the dog raises its back leg in a scratching movement,
it gets so much pleasure from this.
-Barbara Woodhouse

No Dogs

Before we get started on the best places to take your dog, let's get out of the way some of the trails that do not allow dogs:

Bethel Beach Natural Area - *Mathews*
Chincoteague National Wildlife Refuge - *Chincoteague Island*
Hoffler Creek Wildlife Preserve - *Portsmouth*
Voorhees Nature Preserve - *Oak Grove*

O.K. That wasn't too bad. Let's forget about these and move on to some of the great places where we CAN take our dogs around the Tidewater...

The Best Of The Best

- 🐾 **Best place to take your dog for a swim...**
  KIPTOPEKE BEACH STATE PARK

- 🐾 **Best place to take your dog for a one-hour workout...**
  WALLER MILL PARK - LOOKOUT TOWER TRAIL

- 🐾 **Prettiest place to hike with your dog...**
  MARINERS' MUSEUM - NOLAND TRAIL

- 🐾 **Best place to hike with your dog on the beach...**
  HUGHLETT POINT NATURAL AREA - summer
  BACK BAY NATIONAL WILDLIFE REFUGE - off-season

- 🐾 **Best place to take a quick half-hour hike with your dog...**
  CHESAPEAKE ARBORETUM

- 🐾 **Best place to take a historic hike with your dog...**
  GREENSPRINGS GREENWAY (there are so many contenders
  we'll cop out and pick a place you can learn about the entire
  region)

- 🐾 **Best place to hike with your dog in an open field...**
  BELLE ISLE STATE PARK

- 🐾 **Best place to hike with your dog around a lake...**
  OAK GROVE LAKE PARK

*"If there are no dogs in Heaven,
then when I die I want to go where they went."
-Anonymous*

The 33 Best Places To Hike With Your Dog In The Tidewater...

1
First Landing State Park

The Park

In 1873 a U.S. Weather Bureau Observation Center was established at Cape Henry and the next year a U.S. Life Saving Station was built. A small community grew up around the stations and it seemed like the area was about to boom. A group of Norfolk investors formed the Cape Henry Syndicate to encourage development but the popularity of Virginia Beach down the road never materialized.

In 1933 the Syndicate sold 2,000 acres to the Commonwealth of Virginia for $157,000. Federal Civilian Conservation Corps workers arrived and built Seashore State Park, one of Virginia's original six state parks. The park's name was changed in 1997 to First Landing State Park as an homage to the first place where members of the Virginia Company landed in 1607.

Virginia Beach

Phone Number
- (757) 412-2300

Website
- www.dcr.virginia.gov/state_parks/fir.shtml

Admission Fee
- Vehicle entrance fee

Park Hours
- Daylight hours

Directions
- *Virginia Beach*; From I-64, take Northampton Boulevard/U.S. 13 North (Exit 282). Go through 8 lights, then turn right at the Shore Drive/U.S. 60 Exit (last exit before the Chesapeake Bay Bridge Tunnel). Take a right on Shore Drive and go 4.5 miles to the park entrance. For the Trail Center and trails, turn right.

The Walks

The trail system at First Landing State Park, designated as part of the National Recreation Trail System, features 19 miles of dog-friendly hiking. The marquee walk is the *Bald Cypress Trail* that circles a cypress swamp for 1.5 miles, much of the way on elevated boardwalks. Airborne Spanish moss drapes many of the ancient giants. In 1965 the park's natural area was included in the National Register of Natural Landmarks because of its distinction as the northernmost location on the East Coast where subtropical and temperate plants grow and thrive together, darkening the trails with their richness.

Looping off the red-blazed *Bald Cypress Trail* is the 3.1-mile blue *Osmanthus Trail*, named for the American olive tree that grows abundantly on the fringes of the dark lagoon along the trail. Another worthwhile detour from the *Bald Cypress Trail* is the quarter-mile *High Dune Trail* that uses wooden sleeper-steps to ascend a steep, wooded dune. It is easy walking on these

The boardwalks are the dominant feature of the Bald Cypress Trail.

packed sand and soft dirt trails that are further cushioned to the paw by pine straw from majestic loblolly pines. There are gentle undulations that spice up the flat canine hiking along the 8 hiker-only trails and the 6-mile *Cape Henry Multi-Use Trail*.

Trail Sense: Everything is marked, signs abound and most everything leads back to the Trail Center.

Dog Friendliness
Dogs are allowed on the trails and on the beach that stretches along the Chesapeake Bay, except in swimming areas.

Traffic
These are heavily used trails but no horses and no bikes except on the multi-use trail.

Canine Swimming
It doesn't get much better than the Chesapeake Bay for canine aquatics.

Trail Time
Up to a half-day or more.

2
Northwest River Park

The Park

Northwest River Park is the result of the vision of the City of Chesapeake and Mayor Marian Whitehurst in 1977 who purchased three tracts of land to set aside over 700 acres for the enjoyment of nature.

In years gone by the park was the hub of a booming moonshining operation during America's Prohibition in the 1920s - its Moonshine Meadow is not for enjoying celestial lights. Sunken dents in the ground reveal where illegal booze was brewed. Park officials say more than 30 moonshine sites have been discovered on the grounds.

The Walks

This paradise for canine hikers offers about 8 miles of quiet, looping trails through the park on the Northwest River. All the trails more or less connect to the 1.25-mile multi-use *Shuttle Trail* that runs down the spine of the park. Your dog will get about a three-mile loop from either side of the *Shuttle Trail*.

The east side rolls gently through an airy forest on the *Molly Mitchell Trail* and the *Wood Duck Slough Trail*. It is lowlying in spots and suffers from a few too many exposed roots but otherwise is a splendid exploration for your dog. A highlight on this side of the park is a large bald cypress tree several hundred years old on the *Otter Point Trail*.

The opposite side of Northwest River Park is dominated by the 2.5-mile *Indian Creek Trail* that runs past its namesake stream. The destination of choice here is an arched hickory tree hosting a resurrection fern. This fern curls up and

Chesapeake

Phone Number
- (757) 421-7151

Website
- www.chesapeake.va.us/services/depart/park-rec/nwrp/index.shtml

Admission Fee
- None

Park Hours
- 9:00 a.m. to sunset

Directions
- *Chesapeake*; At the end of I-464 stay to left and take Route 168 south. Take Exit 8B, Hillcrest Parkway East (last exit before toll). Turn right onto Battlefield Boulevard and turn left on Indian Creek Road. The park is 4 miles on the right.

turns brown when it is dry and bursts into a healthy green when it rains.

Trail Sense: The trails are not blazed but this is really not a problem. A trail map is available and you will want to hold onto it as you hike. The trailheads are signed.

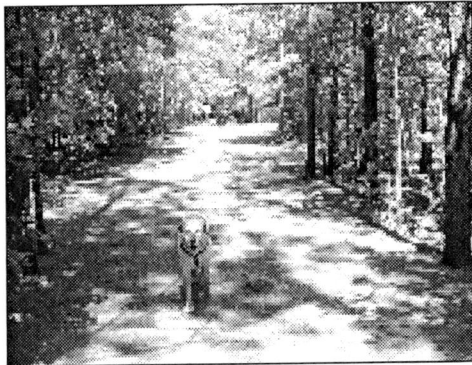

The wide, leafy Shuttle Trail *is a delight for your dog to trot down.*

Dog Friendliness

Dogs are allowed to enjoy the trails and can stay in the campground.

Traffic

Given the quality of the trails this is an underused gem of a park. Bikes are permitted on the multi-use trails.

Canine Swimming

Swimming is not a prime attraction for your dog here. The swampy lake is not inviting. The Northwest River can be accessed for dog paddling in the middle of your loop hike.

Trail Time

A half-day of canine hiking is possible.

"No one appreciates the very special genius of your conversation as a dog does."
-Christopher Morley

3
Hughlett Point Natural Area

The Park

Jessie Dew Ball grew up in Ball's Neck and was the first teacher at the Shiloh Road School (still standing at the corner of Routes 605 & 606). One day she met Alfred I duPont, one of the triumverate of cousins who turned a black powder manufacturer into the world's leading purveyor of chemical products, who was in the neighborhood hunting ducks. Although twenty years her senior, Jessie Ball found she had much in common with the industrialist. The two married and Jessie Ball was to spend much of the rest of her life devoted to philanthropy. She donated to schools and churches in Northumberland County and gave so much to Florida that she and Alfred were named as two of the Most Important Floridians of the 20th Century.

Northern Neck

Phone Number
- None

Website
- www.dcr.virginia.gov/natural_heritage/natural_area_preserves/hughlett.shtml

Admission Fee
- None

Park Hours
- Daylight hours

Directions
- *Kilmarnock*; Go four miles north of town on US 200. Turn right (east) onto Route 606 and go about 2 miles to Route 605. Turn right (south) on Route 605 and go about 2 miles to the preserve parking area on the left.

In 1994 The Virginia Department of Conservation and Recreation won a $654,000 grant to purchase 210 acres on this remote peninsula and save it from waterside development.

The Walks

You will start your exploration with your dog here on a wide, soft and exceedingly agreeable path through a fragrant loblolly forest. Soon you will pop out on the beach of the Chesapeake Bay where you will be excused for thinking you have just landed on Tom Hanks' deserted island in *Cast Away*. Ghost trees and fallen trunks pepper the enchanted shore - ineffective guardians against the relentless Chesapeake wave action.

Follow the wide, sandy woods road as it sails away to your right until you reach the beach. The beach stretches in both directions before you. Although it may not seem obvious, you can close your loop by walking across the exposed beach to your left. Of course, in times of periodic high tide you will have to re-trace your steps - no part of the preserve exceeds 10 feet in elevation. Your dog can also access an observation tower at the edge of the marsh.

Trail Sense: None but that will be ho hindrance.

Dog Friendliness
Dogs are permitted in the preserve.

Traffic
Foot traffic only and usually not much of it.

Canine Swimming
Absolutely, from the beaches of the Chesapeake Bay.

Trail Time
About one hour - but your dog won't be in any hurry to leave.

Isn't this where the S.S. Minnow *came ashore? Where's Gilligan?*

4
Beaverdam Park

The Park

Mordecai Cooke was the earliest English settler of this land, patenting this part of Gloucester in 1652. His descendants established several large estates in the area, including Wareham that includes much of the park property today.

The Beaverdam Reservoir is of recent vintage - in 1990 a newly built earthen dam flooded the open fields and woodlands of Beaverdam Swamp to a depth of 25 feet to stabilize the Gloucester water supply. The 665-acre park surrounds the many tentacled lake.

The Walks

Given just a slender band of land along the lakeshore park officials have succeeded in creating one of the Tidewater's best trail systems. The main multi-use trail stretches 9.5 miles from the main park around the northern edge of the reservoir to Fahy's Road and is used as a stem for a string of loop trails.

Phone Number
- (804) 693-2107

Website
- www.gloucesterva.info/pr/parks/welbvd.htm

Admission Fee
- None

Park Hours
- Vary widely; in summer from 6:00 a.m. to 8:30 p.m.

Directions
- *Gloucester*; From Route 17 turn onto 17 Business into town (Main Street). Turn onto Roaring Springs Raod and follow to the main park at end. For Fahy's Road (Route 606) trailhead, stay on Route 17, turning onto Fahy's Road and continuing three miles.

If you have a car shuttle that journey through thick hardwoods makes for a solid day's outing with your dog but otherwise you have a score of options to craft your canine hiking day. The multi-use trail is hard-packed and stony; the various spur trails are reserved for hikers and more paw-friendly. The two bridges on the route are often used as turn-around points by trail-users; Morgan's Bridge from the main park is a three-mile round-trip and canine adventurers seeking a bigger outing can find a six-mile round trip on the loops at the Route 606 trailhead. Expect rolling terrain throughout.

For a relaxing inroduction to Beaverdam Park's splendors pick up an interpretive brochure and follow the _Lake's Edge Trail_ from the ranger station at the main entrance.

Trail Sense: There are park maps, trail guides, signposts, and blazes.

Dog Friendliness
Dogs are allowed on Beaverdam trails.

Traffic
No bikes or horses are allowed on the hiking trails.

Canine Swimming
Sorry, this is Gloucester's drinking water.

Trail Time
Many hours possible.

Park literature assures you of seeing a Great Blue Heron on your canine hike at Beaverdam Park and so you do.

25

5
Waller Mill
Park

The Park

Dating to Colonial times the Waller family and others ground grain along the Queen's Creek here. In 1911 the Oak Grove School, a one-room Negro school was built and operated for three decades until it was destroyed by lightning on July 28, 1940. Nature accomplished what the federal government would have wrought anyway since two years later the Army Corps of Engineers arrived to build a reservoir to supply water to Camp Peary.

After the war the Waller Mill Reservoir was declared surplus and sold to the City of Williamsburg. Some residents groused about drinking "swamp water" but eventually Williamsburg became the only jurisdiction on the Virginia Peninsula other than Newport News to control its own surface water supply, supplying millions of gallons of water daily to quench the needs of the tourist industry.

In 1963 the earthen dam burst and the reservoir emptied. Lying at the bottom was an old mill stone that has been used to

Williamsburg

Phone Number
- (757) 259-3778

Website
- www.ci.williamsburg.va.us/ dept/rec/parks.htm#waller

Admission Fee
- None to hike, fees for some activities and facilities

Park Hours
- Closing times vary throughout the year; open 7:00 a.m March-October, 8:00 a.m November-February

Directions
- *Williamsburg*; From I-64, exit onto Route 199. Head south on Richmond Road (Route 60) and make a left on Airport Road, Route 645. The park entrance is on the right, just after crossing the water.

symbolize the area's heritage. The park opened in July 1972 with 2,700 acres for recreational use.

The Walks

A trio of shaded trails conspire to make Waller Park a prime destination for canine hikers. You can warm up on the *Shelter Trail* or *Bayberry Trail*, each under a mile and relatively level. The primo trail is the sporty *Lookout Tower Trail* that leads to the other side of the water and the namesake tower, then loops around a picturesque peninsula. The circuit is almost three miles and dishes out plenty of ups and down for your dog throughout. For the most part your dog will be trotting on paw-friendly sand dirt so he can concentrate on those water views.

Trail Sense: The trailheads are marked and accessed from the main parking lot. A trail map is available from the office.

Dog Friendliness
Dogs are permitted to use these trails.

Traffic
The Lookout Tower Trail is not as heavily-trod as the park facilities on the east side of the water. A paved bike path of two miles on an abandoned rail track can be hiked with your dog but you'll be dodging bikes when busy.

Canine Swimming
There is no swimming for your dog in Williamsburg's water supply.

Trail Time
More than one hour.

6
Kiptopeke
State Park

The Park

The site was purchased by the Virginia Ferry Corporation for the northern terminus of the Virginia Beach to Eastern Shore Ferry. In 1949, when the terminus was moved to Cape Charles, the abandoned area was named Kiptopeke Beach in honor of the younger brother of a king of the Accawmack Indians who had befriended early settlers. Kiptopeke means "Big Water." In 1950 the terminus opened after the completion of a $2.75 million pier, promoted as the world's largest and most modern ferry pier. Kiptopeke opened as a state park in 1992.

The Walks

More than four miles of fun trails for your dog traverse this 545-acre

Eastern Shore

Phone Number
- (757) 331-2267

Website
- www.dcr.virginia.gov/state_parks/kip.shtml

Admission Fee
- Vehicle entrance fee

Park Hours
- Daylight hours

Directions
- *Cape Charles*; Kiptopeke is three miles from the northern terminus of the Chesapeake Bay Bridge-Tunnel, on Route 13. Turn west on Route 704; the park entrance is within a half mile.

bayside park. Kiptopeke's nature paths wind over sand dunes through groves of loblolly pines, sassafras and wild-cherry trees. The *Baywoods Trail* slips through an uplands hardwood forest on wide, old field roads and connects with expansive, sandy beaches via an extensive network of wooden boardwalks through the dunes. Your dog will find this hike open and airy as he loops from the farmlands to the beach.

The southern beach is perfect for a canine hike but observe signs designating the special habitat area that is closed to visitors. Bicycle trails are available along the park's entrance road and the *Raptor, Songbird, Chickadee* and *Mockingbird* trails.

Trail Sense: The accurate park map is your main navigational ally.

Dog Friendliness

Dogs are allowed on the trails and in the campground but not in the cabins or yurt.

Traffic

This is a lightly used park and you can expect to be hiking with your dog in relative solitude.

Canine Swimming

There is fantastic swimming for your dog on the sandy beaches (no dogs allowed Memorial Day to Labor Day) of the eastern Chesapeake Bay. Nine World War II-era concrete ships weighing almost 5,000 tons each were placed offshore in 1948 as breakwaters, providing less adventurous dogs a chance to play in gentle waves.

Trail Time

About one hour.

Concrete troop ships from World War II that have been placed in the Chesapeake Bay as a breakwater insure that the waters are always calm at Kiptopeke.

7
Back Bay National Wildlife Refuge

The Park

The lure of the sea has long led humans to try and live in this harsh seaside environment. After their ship wrecked off this coast in the 1800s a settlement of 300 people lived in the Wash Woods section of False Cape. They used flotsam retrieved from the broken ship to build their first homes. The settlers fished and farmed but eventually they drifted away as the shifting sands overwhelmed their village.

Famous hunting clubs for wealthy Philadelphia and New York businessmen dominated the barrier islands through the mid-1900s before over 9,000 acres of coastline were protected. Today, instead of hunting waterfowl here, folks come to count them. As many as 300 species of birds have been tabulated at Back Bay National Wildlife Refuge.

Virignia Beach

Phone Number
- (757) 721-2412

Website
- www.nnparks.com/parks_nn.php

Admission Fee
- Vehicle fee but only when dogs are not allowed in the refuge

Park Hours
- Dawn to dusk

Directions
- *Virginia Beach*; From I-64 take the Indian River Road Exit and go 13 miles to Newbridge Road. After one mile look for Sandbridge Road and turn right. After 3 miles turn right on Sandpiper Road to refuge.

The Walks

There are a cornucopia of canine hiking opportunities at Back Bay. Easy jaunts on two trails lead over to the bay, with plenty of boardwalk to get out into the marshes. The *East Dike* and *West Dike* are fine canine hikes around the refuge impoundments. Your dog will be walking on the typical gravel-and-dirt-road found in our wildlife refuges.

But for many canine hikers the attraction of Back Bay will be four miles of dune-backed, undeveloped beach, heading south. The beach does not actually end there but the refuge does. You can keep hiking with your dog into False Cape State Park and complete a 15-mile loop across the *False Cape Main Trail*, the *Barbour Hill Beach Trail* and back up the refuge's dike trails.

Trail Sense: Some trails are subject to closure for wildlife so if you are planning a special outing with your dog, call ahead. Trail maps are available.

Dog Friendliness

Even though happy visitors with dogs are pictured prominently in refuge publications dogs are only allowed from October 1 to March 31.

Traffic

No horses are allowed in the refuge. You may see flocks of birdwatchers or you may see nobody in your visit. Again, your dog is only allowed in the off-season.

Canine Swimming

Plenty of opportunity.

Trail Time

Many hours to a full day possible.

8
Mariners' Museum– Noland Trail

The Park

In 1930 Archer Huntington, scion to the empire built by Transcontinental Railroad pioneer Collis P. Huntington, founded the Mariners' Museum to tell the story of mankind's relationships with the world's oceans. Huntington came by his love of the sea naturally - his father had also founded the nearby Newport News Shipbuilding and Drydock Company.

Archer Huntington was a scholar with wide-ranging interests. He was the nation's leading authority on all things Spanish and he endowed the museum with a vast collection of objects and books. Outside he sculpted a natural park on the 800 acres of his museum, employing many local shipyard workers in the project. Today, the Mariners' Museum is the largest privately owned park in the country.

Newport News

Phone Number
- (757) 591-7722

Website
- www.mariner.org/

Admission Fee
- None for the park

Park Hours
- 10:00 a.m. to 5:00 p.m Monday-Saturday; 12:00 p.m. to 5:00 p.m. Sundays

Directions
- *Newport News*; From I-64 take exit 258-A. Go 2.5 miles to the intersection of Warwick Boulevard and J. Clyde Morris Boulevard (Avenue of the Arts). Continue straight through the intersection and turn left onto Museum Drive. The entrance is directly ahead.

The Walks

The five-mile plus *Noland Trail* is as pretty an excursion as you can take with your dog in Tidewater Virginia. Technically the 6-foot pathway is constructed of special clay that swells when wet to prevent erosion and serves up a soft walking surface when dry but all your dog will know is that she loves it. The trail is named for Lloyd U. Noland, Jr., whose foundation donated over a million dollars for its construction in 1991 and renovation in 1999. The money comes from the family plumbing and industrial goods supply company.

The *Noland Trail* traces the shoreline of Lake Maury, a 167-acre lake named for famed 19th century oceanographer Matthew Fontaine Maury. Along the way your dog will trot across fourteen bridges through a forest landscape that more resembles a garden.

The park features every species of fern native to Virginia. In the 1930s a hull worker from the Newport News Shipyard named George Mason, a self-taught naturalist, studied the park and found every Virginia fern save four. He collected the absent foursome and transplanted them here. Mason would become park forester.

Trail Sense: Just have your dog follow the crowds if you get worried.

Dog Friendliness

The Huntingtons loved animals - at their estate in Myrtle Beach a bear pen was included on the grounds in addition to the horse stables and dog kennel. Dogs are welcome here.

Traffic

The trail is a magnet for joggers, canine hikers and other users.

Canine Swimming

The trail does touch the lake for easy access to the water at times.

Trail Time

About two hours.

33

9
Hickory Hollow Nature Preserve

The Park

In the 19th century this was the site of a Lancaster County poor house. By the 1960s the poor house was evacuated and the county began selling off timber on the property. Meanwhile, Henry Bashore, a state forester began championing the abandoned site's potential as a natural area. With a team of volunteers, he began to revitalize the woodland and build trails.

For over twenty years area residents quietly enjoyed Bashore's woodland oasis. In 1999, when the County floated plans for an industrial park here Bashore contacted the Audubon Society and triggered grass roots opposition to the destruction of Hickory Hollow.

At a public meeting on the indutrial park proposal, an overflow crowd of 300 showed up to fight the development. The county agreed to sell 254 acres of Hickory Hollow to the Northern Neck Audubon for $320,000.

Northern Neck

Phone Number
- None

Website
- www.northernneckaudubon.org/guide.htm

Admission Fee
- None

Park Hours
- Sunrise to sunset

Directions
- *Lancaster*; The park is west of town adjacent to Lancaster High School. Traveling east on Mary Ball Road (Route 3), the park is on the left after the school, down Regina Road; traveling west, turn right on Regina Road before the school. Preserve parking is on the left.

The Walks

This is classic woodland hiking with your dog - wide, nicely groomed trails over gently rolling terrain. The mixed hardwood and pine forest is still recovering from its earlier days of deprivation so it still has an airy feel about it. There are no great destinations to be had, no lakes or astounding views. Just a great place to get out and hike with your dog.

The main *White Trail* is a lollipop route of almost two miles with several loops and cut-offs along the way. You can bring your dog to Hickory Hollow a dozen times and never hike the same route twice.

Trail Sense: A hand-drawn map is posted at the trailhead information kiosk and trail maps may be available. Out in the woods the trails are blazed and there are signposts at trail junctions - and even a map board in the middle.

Dog Friendliness
Dogs are allowed to enjoy the Hickory Hollow trails.
Traffic
Foot traffic only on these generally lightly used paths.
Canine Swimming
None.
Trail Time
More than one hour.

10
Belle Isle
State Park

The Park

John and Paul Bertrand, brothers, fled from France during the persecutions of Louis XIV and sailed to England where both were clerks in the Church of England. They next emigrated to America. John Bertrand, the elder, settled along the Rappahannock River, acquiring this property in 1692.

Through the centuries the land was owned and divided among several families. Over 300 years afer settlement the Belle Isle Neck became the first property in Virginia to be purchased with funds from the Parks and Recreational Facilities bond. At the time Belle Isle was on the fast track to becoming a luxurious waterfront subdivision but the Commonwealth of Virginia saved those million-dollar views for your dog instead.

Northern Neck

Phone Number
- (804) 462-5030

Website
- www.dcr.virginia.gov/state_parks/bel.shtml

Admission Fee
- Vehicle entrance fee

Park Hours
- Sunrise to sunset

Directions
- *Lancaster*; From the east take Route 3 to Lively and turn left onto Route 201. At the end of the road turn right on Route 354 and left on Route 683 to the park. From the west, turn right on Route 354 from Route 3 and right on Route 683.

The Walks

Belle Isle may be a state park but aside from a windswept picnic pavilion it doesn't look much different than it has since the land was first cleared and the crops first planted. Most of your dog's trotting will be down double-track, packed-clay farm roads. It is an edgy place - hiking on the edge of cropfields, on the edge of marshes, on the edge of light forests...

The star ramble at Belle Isle is the 1.2-mile *Neck Fields Trail* that starts as a hike down a country lane and reaches the preserved pine woods at Brewer's Point at the westernmost spot in the park. Like most of the routes here this is an out-and-back affair with no elevation changes.

Trail Sense: A park map/brochure is available that is mostly accurate. But where is that *Watch House Trail*?

Dog Friendliness
Dogs are allowed to hike through Belle Isle.

Traffic
Hiking trails are open to foot traffic and bicycles; horses are also allowed on many trails. But don't expect to have to elbow your way through these secluded trails.

Canine Swimming
The park features seven miles of shoreline along the Rappahnnock River, Mulberry Creek and Deep Creek.

Trail Time
About one hour.

The wild coastline of the Rappahannock River produces some frisky waves for your dog.

11

Chippokes Plantation State Park

The Park

A dozen years after the English established a beachhead at Jamestown in 1607, Captain William Powell acquired a grant to this property across the James River. He began clearing land and planting crops but was killed in a raid on Chickahominy Indians in 1623. The farm was then called "Chippokes" after a native chief who befriended the colonists and began producing grain, corn, barley and wheat.

Over the years a succession of prominent Virginians owned the plantation as it expanded to 1,683 acres. The last private owner was Victor Stewart, who took over the plows in 1918. After he died his wife donated the farm to the state in 1967 to be used as a park and maintained as a working farm so visitors could experience day-to-day farm life.

And so it remains. Wheat and cotton and corn and peanuts are still grown in the park and the farm is in the running for the title of "Longest Continually Cultivated Farm in America."

Surry

Phone Number
- (757) 294-3625

Website
- http://www.dcr.virginia.gov/state_parks/chi.shtml

Admission Fee
- Vehicle entance fee

Park Hours
- Sunrise to sunset

Directions
- *Surry*; Take Route 10 West through Smithfield. Turn right on Alliance Road (Route 634) and continue to the park four miles on left.

The Walks

This park is sure to bring out the farm dog in your family pet. No groomed trails here but plenty of chance to trot down farm roads almost four centuries old. Under paw will be some paved paths, some gravel and some dirt. And yes, you will be hiking with your dog past cattle and goats and chickens.

One of the best canine hikes here is down the *James River Trail*. About half of its mile length is around open farm fields and half through light woods. Your destination is the James River and a long beach walk. You can use the *College*

38

Run Trail to close a healthy loop or your dog may prefer to just turn around and retrace the pawprints in the sand.

Trail Sense: There are trailhead markers but no trail blazes so grab hold of a park map that is available.

Dog Friendliness

Dogs are allowed throughout the farm and park and in the campground, but not in the cabins.

The Italianate Chippokes Plantation House doubled as a distillery in its early years.

Traffic

All trails are multi-use but no motorized vehicles; this is a lightly visited park when no festivals or special events are scheduled. Horses are allowed in designated areas only.

Canine Swimming

A gently sloping crescent beach at the James River makes this one of the best places for your dog to swim in the Tidewater.

Trail Time

More than one hour.

12
York River State Park

The Park

This land was settled in the 1600s as Taskinas Plantation. Local planters established a tobacco warehouse here where crops could be stored and shipped across the Atlantic Ocean to England. At low tide you can sometimes see the remnants of corduroy roads built of logs where the carts once rolled.

The plantation was later named Croaker for the abundance of bottom-dwelling fish that favor the muddy banks of estuaries such as the Chesapeake Bay. In 1980 York River became a state park to protect the unique estuarine environment along Taskinas Creek and the York River.

Williamsburg

Phone Number
- (757) 566-3036

Website
- www.dcr.virginia.gov/state_parks/yor.shtml

Admission Fee
- Vehicle entance fee

Park Hours
- 8:00 a.m. to dusk

Directions
- *Williamsburg*; From I-64, take the Croaker Exit 231B. Go north on Route 607 (Croaker Road) for one mile, then right on Route 606 (Riverview Road) about one and a half miles to the park entrance. Take a left turn into the park.

The Walks

There is a massive trail system at York River State Park - over 25 miles - but it is all accessed from a single parking lot so most of the trails will only be seen by mountain bikers and equestrians. The one must-do trail in York River for canine hikers is the 1.5-mile *Taskinas Creek Trail* that drops down into the salt marsh and utilizes boardwalks for a close-up experience. Another satisfying loop is the three-quarter mile *Woodstock Pond Trail* that is actually most interesting when it leaves the beaver pond and frolics in the mixed-hardwood forest above.

Serious canine hikers can strap on the backpack and head down the *Backbone Trail* to the multi-use trails. Here, you can choose one of several routes that lead to the park's three miles of frontage on the York River. This is all woods hiking and expect plenty of dips and rises.

40

Trail Sense: Grab a trail map so you can make sense of the park's 16 trails, all of which are enthusiastically blazed.

Dog Friendliness
Dogs are permitted across all trails.

Traffic
The *Marl Ravine Mountain Bike Trail* is a popular test and you will meet riders on the way to its trailhead; also horses. But this is not an overcrowded park by any means.

Canine Swimming
There are a couple of points for your dog to slip into Woodstock Pond and cool off.

Trail Time
More than one hour.

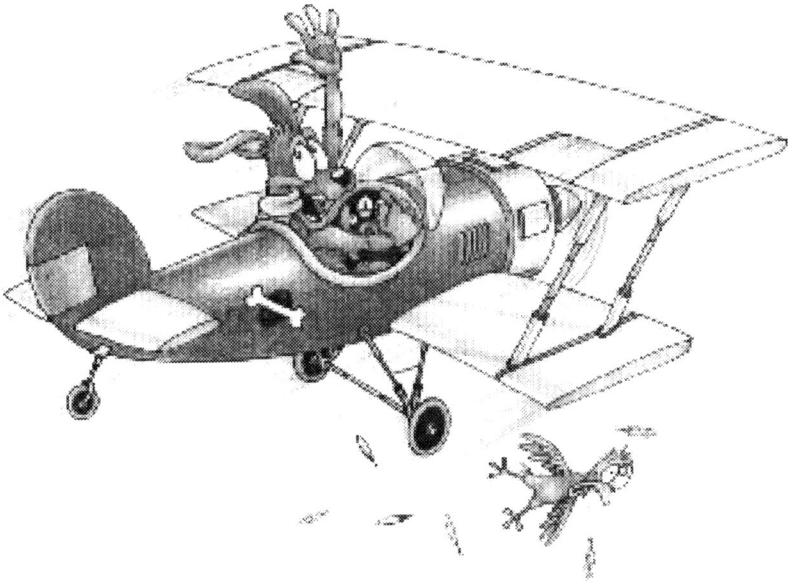

13

Newport News Park

The Park

Faced with growing demand for its drinking water, Newport News created Lee Hall Reservoir. To protect the purity of the water the surrounding watershed was developed into Newport News Park in 1966. The city created plenty of buffering protection - at more than 8,000 acres, Newport News Park is the largest municipal park east of the Mississippi River.

The Walks

Most of the 30-some miles of trail in Newport News Park are on the west side of Lee Hall Reservoir but unless you are staying in the campground you will need to park on the east side and hike across. Aside from the tiny *Lakeside Trail* loop near the park entrance, expect to be out on the trail for at least an hour everytime you set out onto the Newport News Park trail system.

The quickest way to get into the meat of your dog's hiking day is to cross the Dam #1 Bridge. You'll find narrow, soft dirt trails that twist up and down hills through somewhat scruffy woods - all a guarantee of fun for your dog.

One word of warning: you may want to choose a different hiking location after heavy rains. In the wake of flooding from Hurricane Ernesto so many poisonous snakes sought higher ground on the hiking trails that park officials were forced to close the trails for several days.

Trail Sense: A large park map is available and signs at trail junctions get you going on the right path.

Newport News

Phone Number
- (757) 888-3333

Website
- www.nnparks.com/parks_nn.php

Admission Fee
- None

Park Hours
- Sunrise to sunset

Directions
- *Newport News*; From I-64 take Exit 250B North to the immediate intersection with Jefferson Avenue (Route 143). Turn left to the main park entrance on the right and the campground further on across Lee Hall Reservoir.

Bonus

Confederate major general John Bankhead Magruder prepared defensive lines here early in 1862. He also installed levees to flood the lowlands in the event of a Union incurison. The attack came on April 16, 1862, at Dam No. 1, as General McClellan launched his Peninsula Campaign against Richmond. The Federal force was stymied and never again attempted to break through the Confederate defenses along the Warwick River. One of the Union soldiers who died here was William Scott, a private from the 3rd Vermont Regiment. Scott fell asleep while on guard duty and was arrested, tried and sentenced to be shot. At the written request of his unit, Abraham Lincoln pardoned Scott and returned him to his unit to meet his fate here. A highly romanticized poem and silent movie, which had Lincoln riding ten miles to halt the execution, were later made about the incident. Over five miles of continuous earthworks remain in the park and can be seen along the *Twin Forts Loop*, along with interpretive battle markers.

Dog Friendliness

Dogs are welcome to enjoy these trails and can stay in the campground with a current rabies certificate.

Traffic

Road bikes are limited to the *Bikeway* and mountain bikes to Harwood's Mill. The park is big enough that you can expect to go a long time without encountering another trail user.

Canine Swimming

Not here - the lake is for drinking, not swimming.

Trail Time

Many hours possible.

"The greatest pleasure of a dog is that you may make a fool of yourself with him, and not only will he not scold you, but will make a fool of himself too."
- Samuel Butler

14
New Quarter Park

The Park

This land was part of the property purchased in 1709 by Virginia planter Robert "King" Carter, one of Colonial America's most prosperous land barons. For generations slaves tended livestock and harvested timber here. Sloops loaded with tobacco floated down the park waterways out to the Old World.

Near the end of the 20th century York County went looking for its first day-use park. Officials acquired this land between folds of the Queen's Creek and converted a private camping area into a 545-acre county park.

The Walks

An elaborate trail system of 8 short attached loops awaits your dog in this pretty historic park. To complete all 8 loops will cover a bit over three miles as your dog bounds up and down across an ancient seabed. If your dog balks at tackling the entire hiking trail system, it splits at the park office/parking lot. The more attractive set of loops in this case would be Loops 5-8. Along the way you'll pass through mature forests and meadows that have changed little in 75 years.

New Quarter also sports a 5.8-mile *Redoubt Trail* that is designed for mountain bikes and twists hundreds of times through the park woods. Most of the park trails are narrow bands on natural, oyster-shell packed soils. Queen's Creek is also a great place to launch a canoe with your dog.

Williamsburg

Phone Number
- (757) 890-3500

Website
- www.yorkcounty.gov/park-sandrec/parks/new_quarter/1nqp_info.htm

Admission Fee
- None

Park Hours
- 8:00 a.m. to 8:00 p.m. with shorter hours during the winter but you can hike into the park from a parking lot outside the gate on a paved path

Directions
- *Williamsburg*; On Lakeshead Drive, north of the Colonial Parkway. Exit the Parkway at Queen's Lake. From Yorktown, take a right at the stop sign and left on Lakeshead; from Williamsburg take a right at the stop sign and right on Lakeshead.

Trail Sense: You will never find better directional amenities than at New Quarter Park. A color map is available and the trails are color-coded. At each trailhead a mapboard keeps you oriented.

Dog Friendliness
Dogs are allowed on New Quarter trails.

Traffic
Bikes are confined to the *Redoubt Trail* and the hiking trails are not in heavy use.

Canine Swimming
There is no place for your dog to swim along the trails but down at the canoe launch is great dog paddling in the Queen's Creek.

Trail Time
More than one hour.

15
Freedom
Park

The Park

William Ludwell Lee, descended of the Lee family of Stratford, was owner of historic Green Spring Plantation when he died in 1803 at the age of 27 "without issue" (no heirs). In his will Lee freed his slaves who received farmsteads in an area of the 8,000-acre plantation known as the "Hot Water Tract." It was one of America's earliest Free Black Settlements. Throughout the 19th century descendants of the emancipated Green Spring slaves continued to occupy farms in this area.

James City County has poured over $12 million into developing the 689-acre Freedom Park whose mission is to highlight the historical experience of Free Black people here. Archaeological work is ongoing but the recreational amenities of the park have been open since 2002.

Williamsburg

Phone Number
- (757) 259-3200

Website
- www.james-city.va.us/rec-reation/parks-trails/freedom-park.html

Admission Fee
- None

Park Hours
- Gate opens at 7:00 a.m., closing times vary

Directions
- *Williamsburg*; From I-64, exit onto Route 199. Follow Route 199 to Longhill Road and exit onto Longhill. Continue past Lafayette High School to Centerville Road and cross into the park. If traveling on Centerville Road, Route 614, the park is at 5535 Centerville.

The Walks

Driving along the long, winding entrance road to Freedom Park you feel as if you are entering an upscale golf resort. And any golf architect would love to build a course on this tract of woodsy, hilly terrain. But luckily for canine hikers, this is a public park.

The trail system is divided into hiking trails and mountain bike trails. The two hiking loops run in opposite directions from the parking lot and total about one-and-a-half miles. Start on these trails since they are more pleasant than the bike tracks but if your dog is itching for more trail time there are two long

46

Bonus

The British relied mostly on hedges to delineate their fields so the wooden rail fences so symbolic of Colonial farms are most likely an American innovation. The most prevalent type of fence was variously known as the zigzag, snake, worm, or Virginia rail fence, although it may have originated on Long Island, New York. The stacked, self-supporting rails required no joinery or nailing, no elaborate shaping of the rails, and no digging of postholes. Easily built, these fences could be readily dismantled and reassembled elsewhere. Your dog can examine a typical Virginia rail fence at Freedom Park.

loops and a short biking loop you can try.

This is all shady, undulating canine hiking. And the wildflowers are not restricted to the Williamsburg Botanical Garden at the entrance.

Trail Sense: A trail map is available at the parking lot and do not let it go. The trails are marked only at junctions and there is a stray unmarked trail or two out there.

This Virginia rail fence in the meadow at Freedom Park is part of the effort to interpret the historic Free Black Settlement here.

Dog Friendliness
Dogs are allowed on the Freedom Park trails.

Traffic
Foot traffic only on the hiking trails.

Canine Swimming
The various streams are deep enough only for minnows to swim.

Trail Time
Several hours possible.

16
Wahrani
Nature Trail

The Park

This was originally the land of
the Powhatan Confederacy until English settlement and the formation of
New Kent in the late 1600s. George
Washington wed Martha Dandridge
Custis in New Kent and the first couple
often attended the Upper Church of
Blisland Parish that was built here
in 1703. Also known as Warreneye
Church, it was in ruins by the time
the Richmond Militia used it as an
encampment during the War of 1812.

For many years the Chesapeake
Corporation owned this property and
constructed a private trail system in the
woods used as a tree nursery. In 2003
New Kent obtained the 150-acre woodland and renamed the park "Wahrani"
to honor the region's Powhatan heritage.

Middle Peninsula

Phone Number
- None

Website
- None

Admission Fee
- None

Park Hours
- Sunrise to sunset

Directions
- *New Kent*; From I-64 take
Route 33 East. The parking lot
for the nature park will be on
the right hand side, set back
and somewhat obscured by
the trees while traveling at
high speed.

The Walks

This is a wild and wooly canine hike that twists and turns through small
ravines and up and around frequent knolls. The sporty track is a bit like riding
a good rollercoaster where you want to jump back on as soon as the ride finishes.
The trail system, however, is confusing, so come with a mind to explore with
your dog.

No map is currently available at the trailhead but as you start into the
woods you are greeted by three bright colors of large plastic triangles, newly
put in place by New Kent. You think the trail will be obvious but you would be
wrong. The old trail blazes from the former private trail show up in places and
the triangles disappear.

The trails are essentially a set of stacked loops and the easiest way to navigate is to keep turning in whatever direction you begin at the first junction to circle the park property. Still, downed trees and detours may stop you. Chances are your dog will never notice as he races to the next ridge, eager to discover what awaits. The all natural dirt trails are completely wooded and can get narrow in places.

Trail Sense: The trails are blazed but do not instill confidence.

Dog Friendliness

Dogs are allowed to enjoy these trails.

Traffic

This is a lightly used park.

Canine Swimming

At most your dog may find some splashing in a seasonal stream.

Trail Time

More than one hour.

17
Grandview Nature Preserve

The Park

Winslow Lewis was a sea captain turned engineer and inventor in the early 19th century. He created a new lighting system based on Argand oil lamps and in 1812 the United States Congress awarded him a contract to equip all American lighthouses with his lamps.

Lewis was soon building most of the new lighthouses in the country. He developed standard cookie-cutter plans for brick lighthouses in five sizes. He came here in 1829 to construct a 30-foot tower on Grandview Beach. The Back River Lighthouse, keeper's quarters and a 144-foot bridge over the marsh all cost less than $5,000.

In reality, Winslow Lewis knew little about accepted engineering standards and most of his lighthouses

Hampton

Phone Number
- None

Website
- None

Admission Fee
- None

Park Hours
- Sunrise to sunset

Directions
- *Hampton*; From I-64 take Exit 263B onto Mercury Boulevard North. Take a left on Foxhill Road and a left on Beach Road. Continue on Beach Road for 2.6 miles, and then turn left on State Park Drive. Park along the road and walk to the entrance at the end of State Park Drive.

were poorly constructed or too short for their intended purpose. Most had to be replaced but the Back River Light soldiered on, illuminating the entrance to the Chesapeake Bay until it was decommisioned in 1936.

The historic lighthouse was left to deteriorate, overlooked by preservationists. In 1956 a hurricane washed it away. All that remains of the Back River Light, once built safely inland, is a jumble of rocks many yards offshore. Back on land, the Commonwealth of Virginia has created a 578-acre preserve at the north end of Hampton.

The Walks

You bring your dog to Grandview to hike on its more than two miles of white sand beach. A short trail through the marsh and dunes curves to the Chesapeake but you can no longer hike on the dunes so the beach is it. And that's plenty for most dogs.

Trail Sense: Up and down the beach until you can go no more.

There is always a surprise for your dog to discover at Grandview Beach.

Dog Friendliness

Dogs are not allowed in the Preserve from May 15 to September 15.

Traffic

This is a secluded bay-front beach, especially for dogs who are only allowed in the off-season.

Canine Swimming

The gentle surf will beckon even the most timid of dogs into the water.

Trail Time

A half-day of canine beach hiking is possible.

18
Yorktown Battlefield

The Park

By 1781, fighting in the Revolutionary War had continued for the better part of six years with no real resolution in sight. The British, frustrated by Nathaneal Greene's continuing efforts to thwart their southern expedition, contented themselves with raiding parties in the Colonies.

In the summer of 1781 Lord Cornwallis set about fortifying Yorktown and Gloucester Point but on September 5 the French Navy and Admiral Francois de Grasse engaged a British reinforcement fleet and inflicted enough damage to force the British Navy back to New York.

General George Washington followed the French fleet down the coast with an Army of more than 17,000 men and laid siege to Yorktown. Without reinforcements, the 8,300 British soldiers had no choice but to surrender 19 days later, triggering talks that would end the American Revolution.

Yorktown

Phone Number
- (757) 898-3400

Website
- www.nps.gov/archive/colo/Yorktown/ythome.htm

Admission Fee
- Vehicle entrance fee

Park Hours
- Sunrise to sunset

Directions
- *Yorktown*; Yorktown is part of the Colonial National Historic Park. From US 17 take the Colonial Parkway to the Visitor Center.

The Walks

Yorktown doesn't maintain formal hiking trails - the park is traversed by two driving loops - but there are plenty of opportunities to explore the battlefield with your dog on foot. The historic site is graced by an abundance of trees and rolling hills in a park-like setting. Turnouts and wayside exhibits afford easy access to these canien leg stretchers.

A prime stop is at the reconstructed redoubts 9 and 10, which anchored the east end of the British line. The Americans under Alexander Hamilton assaulted Redoubt 10 and the French stormed Redoubt 9. After intense hand-to-hand fighting both earthen forts were overrun in less than thirty minutes.

The *Battlefield Tour* is a 7-mile driving loop that could actually be hiked with your dog; traffic is generally light and there is plenty of room to step off the paved roadway if necessary. Footpaths also connect to the hiking trail system of the adjacent Newport News Park.

Trail Sense: A detailed park map brochure is available to interpret the historic site.

Dog Friendliness
Dogs are welcome on the grounds of Yorktown Battlefield.

Traffic
Except on special event days park traffic is typically light.

Canine Swimming
Not here.

Trail Time
More than an hour is possible.

19
Great Dismal Swamp NWR

The Park

How dismal is the Great Dismal Swamp? Unlike elsewhere in the Tidewater there was no need for English settlers to force the Indian tribes off the land - they had left already.

George Washington was one of the first to take an interest in the money-making possibilities of the swamp. He visited in 1763 and subsequently organized the Dismal Swamp Land Company to drain and log portions of the swamp. Over the next 200 years all of the cypress and Atlantic white cedar forests would be logged at least once.

Establishment of the refuge began in 1973 when the Union Camp Corporation donated 49,100 acres of land to The Nature Conservancy. This land was then conveyed to the Department of the Interior, and the refuge was officially established through The Dismal Swamp Act of 1974.

Suffolk

Phone Number
- (757) 986-3705

Website
- www.fws.gov/northeast/greatdismalswamp/

Admission Fee
- None

Park Hours
- Sunrise to sunset

Directions
- *Suffolk*; Head south of town on Route 13 to Route 32 for 4.5 miles and follow brown refuge signs.

The Walks

If you are looking for a place to disappear with your dog on a hike for hours, this is it. During its logging years, over 140 miles of roads were constructed through the Dismal Swamp. The best place to launch your adventure is the parking lot at the end of Jericho Lane, off Route 642. Your dog will be hiking on firm sand/dirt roads, level and easy everywhere. Shade is at a premium on hot days so pack plenty of water for your outing. You can create a hiking loop from the several ditches that join at Jericho Lane.

The refuge has also developed an interpretive trail at the site of Washington's former camp, Dismal Town. An extensive boardwalk, nearly a mile long with a couple of spurs, snakes through the heart of the swamp.

Trail Sense: Useful information boards can be consulted at the trailheads but don't try to take your dog into the swamp without a map - it is a long way before the ditch/trails reach junctions in the 109,000-acre refuge.

Your dog will find more amenities for hikers at Great Dismal Swamp than is normally found at national wildlife refuges.

Dog Friendliness
Dogs are welcome to hike through the refuge.

Traffic
Bikes can use the trails but don't be surprised if you don't meet another soul - human or canine - all day.

Canine Swimming
Lake Drummond is the largest natural doggie swimming hole in Virginia. The ditches along the trail often contain water that can be refreshing on a warm hike.

Trail Time
Many hours possible.

20
Sandy Bottom Nature Park

The Park

Although the Big Bethel Road that runs by the park has been carrying traffic between Hampton Roads and Yorktown for nearly 300 years urban development passed this area by. That changed dramatically in the 1950s when the Virginia Department of Transportation started mining sand needed to build I-64.

When VDOT finally left twenty years later rain and groundwater had filled many of the abandoned water pits. The vacated property became a magnet for four-wheelers and illegal dumping. Need to get rid of that old clunker in your front yard? Hey, I know a place...

In 1994, the City of Hampton approached VDOT with an ambitious plan to create a park on the scarred site. They came away with a deed for 250 acres and acquired almost 200 more from private property holders. With the degradation stopped, nature reclaimed the park with a vengeance and the public has responded in kind - park planners hoped to attract usage rates for the new park of around 70,000 and instead more than a half-million folks visit Sandy Bottom Nature Center every year.

Hampton

Phone Number
- (757) 825-4657

Website
- www.hampton.gov/sandybottom

Admission Fee
- None for hiking

Park Hours
- Sunrise to sunset

Directions
- *Hampton*; At the corner of Hampton Roads Center Parkway (West and Big Bethel Road (Route 600). From I-64 take Exit 261A to Big Bethel Road. Entrances are straight through the intersection or to the right on Big Bethel Road.

The Walks

Sandy Bottom Nature Park is loaded with short trails that pile upon one another around two centerpiece lakes and wetlands. The *Lake Trail* hugs the shore on paw-friendly pine straw and dirt for most of its journey as it ducks in and out of light woods. This is easy trotting for any dog and don't be surprised

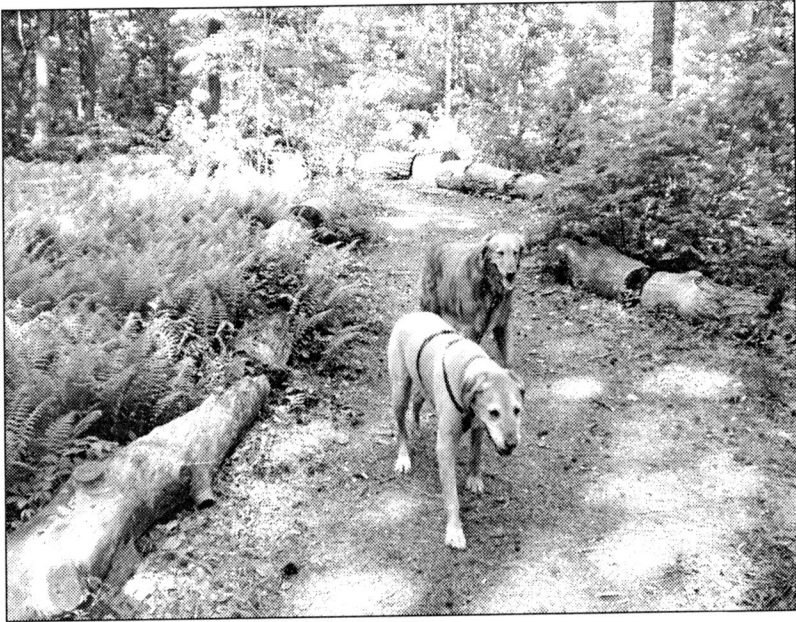

The **Wood Duck Trail** *is lined with huge chunks of timber - no excuse for not following this trail.*

if you wind up visiting all the park trails during your visit; the total mileage is a bit over six. Prepare your dog for the noise, however. The din of traffic from I-64 and passing jets is ever-present.

Trail Sense: A trail map is available and signposts mark trailheads and junctions - blazes are superfluous here.

Dog Friendliness
Dogs are welcome on the trails and in the campground.

Traffic
This is a busy park; bikes are allowed on some trails.

Canine Swimming
There are spots along the *Lake Trail* where your dog can slip into the water for a swim.

Trail Time
An hour or more is possible.

21
Westmoreland State Park

The Park

On June 15, 1936 Virginia became the first state to open an entire park system on a single day when it cut the ribbon on six facilities across the state. Westmoreland, on the Potomac River sandwiched between the birthplaces of George Washington and Robert E. Lee, was one of those six original parks.

The Civilian Conservation Corps, employed by Franklin Delano Roosevelt during the Depression, built the park, hand-digging the trails and roads. Most of the handsome stone-and-wood buildings are still in use, the most fabulous among them the historic Conference center, nestled atop the 150-foot Horsehead Cliffs overlooking the scenic Potomac River.

Northern Neck

Phone Number
- (804) 493-8821

Website
- www.dcr.virginia.gov/state_parks/wes.shtml

Admission Fee
- Vehicle entrance fee

Park Hours
- Sunrise to sunset

Directions
- *Montross*; The park is on the north side of Route 3, six miles west of Montross. The park entrance road is Route 347.

The Walks

A labyrinth of short, interconnecting trails sweep up from the Potomac River through the campsites to Big Meadows. All told, seven named paths cover about six miles. Most of the going is easy for your dog under a leafy canopy - unless you are moving between the Potomac River and tops of the cliffs. The newest trail in the park, the *Beach Trail*, is a round-trip of about one mile that features a drop of more than 100 feet, 30 to 45 degree inclines, benches at the halfway point and offers a stunning view of the Potomac River. Most of the park trails are not that extreme. You can also hike along the sandy/rocky beach with your dog for quite a distance as well.

Trail Sense: A park map/brochure points leads the way and the trails are signed and marked.

Dog Friendliness

Dogs are allowed on the trails, in the campground, and along the beach but not in the bathing areas.

Traffic

The hiking trails are for foot traffic only.

Canine Swimming

Absolutely, plenty of access to the Potomac River.

Trail Time

More than an hour.

There is good canine swimming beneath the cliffs in the Potomac River.

22
Chesapeake Arboretum

The Park

In 1985, Abby Hughes and Wade Long, both Chesapeake Master Gardeners, hatched a plan for a city arboretum that would be a cross between a botanical garden and natural classroom. For years the nonprofit Chesapeake Arboretum Inc. searched for a suitable location but it wasn't until 1996, thanks to a recent city ordinance requiring developers to dedicate natural features in exchange for the ability to build higher concentrations of homes. Just such a natural area was preserved in Oak Grove along a meandering stream and the 47-acre Chespaeake Arboretum became a reality. Most of the property survives in a mature hardwood forest but 5 acres have been dedicated to demonstration and research gardens.

Chesapeake

Phone Number
- (757) 382-7060

Website
- www.chesapeakearboretum.com

Admission Fee
- None

Park Hours
- Daylight hours

Directions
- *Chesapeake*; From I-64 take Exit 290 a/b for Battlefield Boulevard (Route 168) South for 2.25 miles to Gainsborough Square. Turn left at the light and continue .2 miles until the road ends. Turn left onto Oak Grove Road and another immediate left into the Arboretum parking lot at 624 Oak Grove Road.

The Walks

The Chesapeake Arboretum group wanted a location in a residential area that would afford easy access to the most people and they certainly found it. This linear park stretches for more than one mile, squeezed in between thousands of homes. Step ten paces off the trail at almost any time and your dog is liable to find himself in someone's backyard. But the magic of this place is that you never know it on your canine hike.

The woods are so thick and varied - you could spend hours trying to locate the 100 or so identified species of trees and bushes - that you feel as if you are in a much larger woodland. The richness of the flora promotes almost a tunnel effect in places where the trails narrow.

Your dog will find the going easy on soft dirt and woodchip paths. All the terrain in the Arboretum is flat. For the most part the trail works along both sides of the brook for a total loop of over two miles. But the water is crossed by five bridges so you can give your dog any length of outing here.

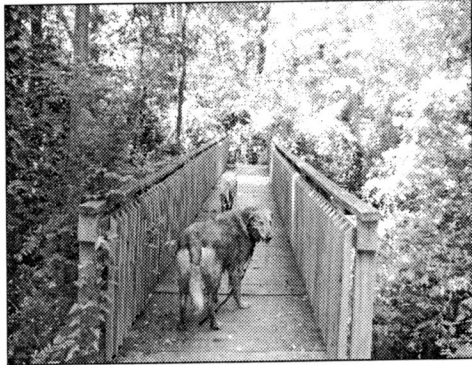

These sturdy bridges enable you to craft any length of canine hike with your dog at Chesapeake Arboretum.

Trail Sense: A detailed trail map is available at the parking lot kiosk.

Dog Friendliness

Dogs are welcome in the Arboretum and poop bags are provided.

Traffic

Foot traffic only. The trail system has ten access points from the surrounding neighborhoods so an empty parking lot at the Arboretum doesn't mean you have the trails to yourself.

Canine Swimming

A neighborhood retaining pond located on the east side of the trail will do the trick. It is not pretty but your dog won't notice on a hot day.

Trail Time

Up to an hour or more is possible.

"*Dogs' lives are too short. Their only fault, really.*"
-Agnes Sligh Turnbull

23
George Washington Birthplace

The Park

The Washington family saga in America began in 1657 when seafaring John Washington tarried in the Tidewater, befriended Nathaniel Pope and married Pope's daughter, Anne. The couple was given 700 acres on Mattox Creek as a wedding gift to start a tobacco farm. John eventually acquired more than 10,000 acres.

John Washington's grandson, Augustine claimed his inheritance on Bride's Creek and purchased more than 1,000 more acres on Pope's Creek. He fathered four children by Jane Butler who died at the age of 30 in 1729.

Northern Neck

Phone Number
- (804) 224-1732

Website
- www.nps.gov/gewa/

Admission Fee
- Individual entrance fee

Park Hours
- 9:00 a.m to 5:00 p.m.

Directions
- *Washington's Birthplace*; on the north side of Route 3, west of Montross.

Washington remarried a year later, taking as his bride Mary Ball, an orphaned daughter of a prominent planter. Their first child, George, was born in 1732 in the manor house at Pope's Creek. Although the family moved away when he was not yet four, George returned many times as an adolescent to work the family plantation.

On Christmas Day, 1779, while Washington was busy guiding the Continental Army, the manor house of his birth burned. It was never rebuilt. The birthplace was excavated in 1936 and the foundations preserved. Its location and dimensions are indicated by an oyster shell outline. A typical Tidewater house of the upper classes of the 1700s has been constructed on the property as a memorial to President George Washington.

The Walks

Teh 538-acre national monument has been developed as a representative tobaco plantation and there is plenty of room to roam with your dog. Packed gravel paths lead around the house, fields, groves of trees and gardens.

A wooded nature trail runs for a mile on a wide, leaf-littered natural surface through a coastal mixed pine forest. Plus, there is plenty of grass for your dog to trot on. And you can hike with your dog along the Potomac River beach. All in all, not a bad day for your dog.

Trail Sense: A park map/brochure is available.

Dog Friendliness
Dogs are allowed around the grounds at George Washington Birthplace National Monument.

Traffic
The *Nature Trail* is one of the last places visitors head.

Canine Swimming
The Potomac River can host some dog paddling.

Trail Time
More than one hour.

"Any man who does not like dogs and want them does not deserve to be in the White House."
-Calvin Coolidge

24
Greensprings Greenway

The Park

The Greensprings Greenway steps above its cousins in the category of walking/jogging paths developed in suburban residential developments. The care in its planning and construction make the Greenway a destination for adventurous canine hikers. For instance, wildflowers located in the path of the trails were relocated and transplanted so the entire trail was designated a wildflower sanctuary. It continues to receive transplants from other developments within the county. The trail is stuffed with so many interpretive signs that you almost don't have to visit neighboring Jamestown and Williamsburg to learn about the area's pivotal American history.

The Walks

The central feature of the Greensprings Greenway is a 34-acre beaver pond that attracts so many nesting birds that it has earned a place on the

Williamsburg

Phone Number
- (757) 259-3200

Website
- www.james-city.va.us/rec-reation/parks-trails/green-springs-trail.html

Admission Fee
- None

Park Hours
- Sunrise to sunset

Directions
- *Williamsburg*; The trail is behind Jamestown High School at 3751 John Tyler Highway, Route 5, west of town. A trailhead parking lot has been proposed beyond the tennis courts at the end of Eagle Way opposite Greensprings Plantation Drive but to date has not been realized. Until then, parking is available during non-school hours but dogs are not allowed on school grounds.

Virginia Bird and Wildlife Trail. The *Main Loop* circles this wetland on a wide, soft dirt path that will delight any dog. You'll find only the slightest of elevation changes as you hike through light woods. This canine hike clocks in at just under two miles; other loops are proposed for development but for now the additional trail time available at Greensprings can best be regarded as exercise hikes, which isn't a bad thing either.

Trail Sense: A trail map can be had at the trailhead.

This arched tree survived an ice storm to soldier on in a grotesque form.

Dog Friendliness
Dogs are allowed to hike on the Greenway but not on the Jamestown High School fields.

Traffic
Like any neighborhood walking path if you can come on weekdays between 9:00 and 5:00 you will avoid the majority of joggers, cyclists, and strollers.

Canine Swimming
This is a hiking, not a swimming, exploration.

Trail Time
About one hour.

25
Lone Star Lakes Park

The Park

From the 1920s to the 1950s Lone Star Industries gouged marl - a main ingredient in cement - from the ground here. In the 1980s the firm sold the property to Suffolk city for $1.5 million. Over the years Lone Star had filled some of its pits with water and stocked them for VIP fishermen. The city developed its new 1,063-acre park around the "lakes" dug by Lone Star.

Today Lone Star Lakes Park is a paradise for fishermen. All 11 lakes and two creeks are fishable and the healthy mix of salt and fresh waters produces a richly diverse piscine menu.

Suffolk

Phone Number
- (757) 255-4308

Website
- www.suffolk.va.us/parks/ls.html

Admission Fee
- None to hike

Park Hours
- Sunrise to sunset

Directions
- *Suffolk*; From I-464 take US 17 North. Turn left on Crittenden Road (Route 628) to its end at Route 125. Turn right and the park entrance will be on the right beyond Crystal Lake.

The Walks

The best hike with your dog at Lone Star Lakes Park is the *Archery Trail* that spins around a small wooded island. This wide path is soft dirt under paw and shady above. Of course, you don't want to set out on this one-mile loop unless you are 1000% positive the archery range is not in use. Another nature trail is the shortish *Double Decker Trail* that loops to the rise of a small knoll but many canine hikers just use the unpaved park roads for their dog's outing here. It is one-way and unpaved as it makes a leisurely tour around several lakes.

Trail Sense: A park map is posted at the information boards.

Dog Friendliness
Dogs are welcome to hike in the park and also to go fishing with you.
Traffic
Most of the traffic is out on the water. Horses have their own trail in the northern section of the park.
Canine Swimming
Water, water everywhere and not a drop to swim in. Not really but most of the lakeshores are mucky. That won't stop water-loving hounds, however.
Trail Time
More than an hour is possible.

26
Oak Grove Lake Park

The Park

Oak Grove Lake Park began life as a borrow pit for the construction of I-464. When the highway was finished the Virginia Department of Transportation gave the big hole in the ground to the Chesapeake Department of Parks and Recreation with the stipulation that it be developed into a park within the year of its April 1999 donation.

The department left the area's trees intact and created a passive recreation park for joggers and hikers and the Department of Public Works set about to neutralize the acidic water that would become Oak Grove Lake. The lake's waters have since become so clean that it is now stocked with bass and bluegill and there are proposals to dump sand on the east shore and create a beach.

Chesapeake

Phone Number
- None

Website
- www.chesapeake.va.us/services/depart/park-rec/oakgrovepark.shtml

Admission Fee
- None

Park Hours
- Sunrise to sunset

Directions
- *Chesapeake*; From I-64 take Exit 290B for Battlefield Boulevard South (Route 168 Business). Turn right onto Volvo Parkway and right onto Byron Street to park (signed).

The Walks

Oak Grove Lake Park features about 130 acres, evenly divided between the 65-acre lake and 65 acres of woodlands and wetlands. A 1.5-mile trail circumnavigates the water, constructed partly on the roads used by earthhaulers to move sand from the borrow pit to the highway construction.

Your canine hike begins on a wide, beautiful piney entrance path that leads to the lake. The circuit around the lake isn't as splendid as that introduction but it is on paw-friendly natural surfaces and is shady most of the way around. It a flat, easy trot. The only downside to a canine hike in Oak Grove Lake Park is the unrelenting noise of the traffic roaring past on the Chesapeake Expressway.

Trail Sense: None but none needed.

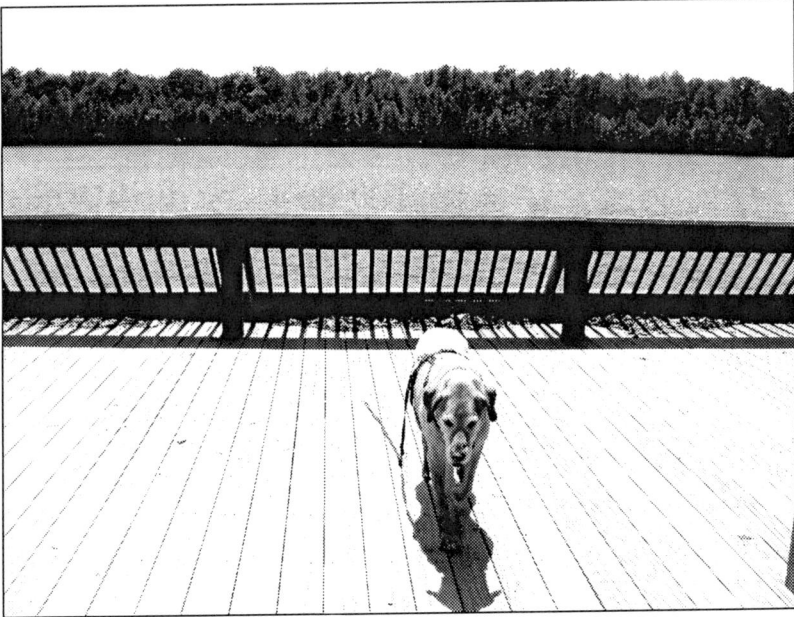

Your dog will find the viewing platforms at Oak Grove Lake Park first-rate.

Dog Friendliness
Dogs are frequent users of this park.

Traffic
This is a good place to come for a communal dog walk.

Canine Swimming
Some of the area's best doggie dips are taken in Oak Grove Park.

Trail Time
About one hour.

27

Eastern Shore of Virginia NWR

The Park

Captain John Smith seems to have been suitably impressed when he first sailed by this area in the early 1600s. He wrote, "...a faire Bay compassed but for the mouth with fruitful and delightsome land...Heaven and earth never agreed better to frame a place for man's habitation." These first settlers farmed the uplands and hunted and fished in the wetlands.

This location at the mouth of the Chesapeake Bay was also coveted by the military for its strategic value. At the beginning of World War II Fort John Custis was garrisoned, named for a powerful member of the colonial Virginia governor's Council from 1727 to 1749. The Air Force occupied the base until 1981 when the land was turned over to the Government Services Agency.

Three years later the U.S. Fish & Wildlife Service purchased the land for one of its more than 500 national wildlife refuges. The base had contained 63 buildings but most were removed to return the land to its natural beauty.

Eastern Shore
Phone Number - (757) 331-2760
Website - www.fws.gov/northeast/easternshore/
Admission Fee - None
Park Hours - Sunrise to sunset
Directions - *Cape Charles*; On the eastern shore, the refuge is the first right after the northern terminus of the Chesapeake Bay Bridge-Tunnel, on Route 13.

The Walks

The hiking with your dog is relaxed and easy at Eastern Shore of Virginia National Wildlife Refuge. There are two short one-way trails, the *Butterfly Trail* and the *Wildlife Trail*, both about a half-mile long. Each is flat and open, exposed to the ocean breezes.

On the *Butterfly Trail* your dog will spend most of the time on paw-friendly mown grass when it is dry. On wet days it can be too soft for boot and paw.

On the *Wildlife Trail* you'll spend time in a maritime forest under regal loblolly pines. You can also hike with your dog along the ocean marshes on the uncrowded refuge roads.

Trail Sense: A refuge map is available to guide you around.

These imposing bunkers once housed 16-inch guns to protect the Atlantic coastline during World War II.

Dog Friendliness
Dogs are welcome to trot around the refuge.

Traffic
Most days you are likely to be alone with your dog except in the fall when millions of birds arrive. The Eastern Shore has the greatest diversity of migratory birds on the Atlantic Flyway north of Florida.

Canine Swimming
Your dog will need to stick to hiking in the refuge.

Trail Time
About one hour.

"Dog. A kind of additional or subsidiary Deity designed to catch the overflow and surplus of the world's worship."
-Ambrose Bierce

28
Bush Mill Stream Natural Area

The Park

The Atlantic coastal plain stretches inland 90 miles from the ocean and is broken by hundreds of marshes, tidal rivers and creeks. The Bush Mill Stream Natural Area preserves a classic example of the genre at the headwaters of the Great Wicomico River where fresh and salt waters tango. The slightly brackish waters are super-rich nurseries for blue crabs and Atlantic menhaden and many other aquatic species.

This property was acquired with Virginia citizens' contributions to the Open Space Recreation and Conservation Fund, and with assistance from the Northern Neck of Virginia Audubon Society and from The Nature Conservancy.

Northern Neck

Phone Number
- None

Website
- www.dcr.virginia.gov/natural_heritage/documents/pg-bushmill.pdf

Admission Fee
- None

Park Hours
- Sunrise to sunset

Directions
- *Heathsville*; Take Route 642 East off Route 201 (there is a brick church and a "nature preserve" sign rather than a road sign). Go 0.3 mile to the preserve entrance on the left. The parking area is 0.1 mile down the gravel entrance.

The Walks

The *Deep Landing Trail* is not long - a tick over a half-mile to the observation platform at the end - but it packs a bit of a punch, dropping some 100 feet in short bursts. The change in elevation will be evident by the vegetation as you hike with your dog here. After starting in a thick understory of mountain laurel the woods begin to thin out as you climb down into a typical oak-hickory-beech climax forest and the views lengthen. As you reach the bottom, water-loving species such as swamp tupelo and red maple begin to dominate.

You can add variety and extra time to your outing here by using the *Heron Trail* on your return trip. This side trail loops around the side of the slopes to stop at an observation point up the marshes of Bush Mill Stream. There are hundreds of feet of soft alluvial soil under your dog's feet in the natural area so she can be assured of a comfortable trot.

Trail Sense: There is no trail map available at the trailhead but you can just follow the *Deep Landing Trail* until it ends; it is well-blazed and so are the turn-offs onto the *Heron Trail*.

Dog Friendliness
Dogs are welcome to hike the natural area.

Traffic
No bikes and no horses - the parking lot scarcely has room for six cars so don't expect any people or dogs either.

Canine Swimming
Yes, the trail does provide access to Bush Mill Creek that is deep enough for a refreshing swim.

Trail Time
About one hour.

The upper slopes of Bush Mill Stream Natural Area are characterized by luxurient stands of mountain laurel.

29
Mount
Trashmore

The Park

In the late 1960s, Roland E. Dorer, then-director of the State Department of Health, Insect and Vector Control, proposed an innovative plan to convert a city landfill into a vibrant green park. 640,000 tons of trash were soon covered with dirt and sod. The hill topped 60 feet and rivalled the beach dunes as Virginia Beach's highest elevation. The hole used to dig the dirt was filled with water. In 1974 the 165-acre park opened and became a beloved destination for a million visitors a year.

By the early 2000s the mountain of trash was in dire need of recapping. The city closed the park for two years and poured $2 million into its renovation. More than 50,000 wetlands plants were placed around the lake to filter the water and protect the banks from erosion. A new impervious liner was installed over the entire mountain to eliminate seeps. It was all topped with 18 acres of Bermuda sod.

Virginia Beach

Phone Number
- (757) 473-5237

Website
- www.virginia.org/site/description.asp?AttrID=24654

Admission Fee
- None

Park Hours
- 7:30 a.m. to sunset

Directions
- *Virginia Beach*; The park is at 310 Edwin Drive. Exit I-264 onto Route 410, South Indpendence Road. Make a left on South Boulevard and your fourth right into the park on Mount Trashmore Park Road.

Mount Trashmore became a model for dealing with trash across the country and another landfill-to-park project has been planned for Virginia Beach. This one is supposed to contain ski runs on artificial snow.

The Walks

The main trail at Mount Trashmore is a 1.5-mile asphalt walking path that surrounds the park. There is no shade for your dog when it's hot but you get plenty of long views on a clear day. If that isn't enough of a workout for your dog you can spend time going up and down the 72-step staircase that climbs to the top of the hill.

Trail Sense: You won't need to rely on your dog's nose to find your way around Mount Trashmore.

Dog Friendliness
Dogs are allowed to romp in the park.

Traffic
Mount Trashmore is a busy park with plenty of trail users.

Canine Swimming
There are two lakes in the park but they have been closed periodically due to run-off from the underlying trash heap. Presently the lakes are stocked with freshwater fish so it may be safe for your dog.

Trail Time
About one hour.

30
Gloucester Point Beach Park

The Park

Gloucester Point puts the squeeze on the York River so that is has always been a popular crossing point. It was fortified as early as 1667 and in 1707, Gloucestertown was laid out above the thriving tobacco port at the geographic point. Later, Gloucester was a central player in the region's bustling daffodil trade in the late 1800s. That heritage is celebrated the first Saturday in April during the annual Daffodil Festival.

On September 18, 2003, Hurricane Isabel made landfall on the Atlantic Coast. Although only a Category 2 storm, Isabel brought such heavy rains and storm surge that Virginia suffered its most extensive power outages ever. Isabel's surge reached nearly 10 feet above low tide, mere inches below the highest levels on record from the historic 1933 blow. Gloucester Point took a direct hit and parts of the park were closed all the way into 2006.

Middle Peninsula

Phone Number
- None

Website
- www.gloucesterva.info/pr/parks/gpb.htm

Admission Fee
- None

Park Hours
- Sunrise to sunset

Directions
- *Gloucester Point*; The park is at the foot of the eastern terminus of the Coleman Bridge. If crossing the bridge, turn right at the first stop light onto Lafayette Height Drive (left if coming from the west). Make a right at Greate Road at the end of Lafayette and continue to the park at the end of Greate.

The Walks

The *Point Walk* at Gloucester Beach is neither a long nor taxing hike with your dog but it is scenic and informative. The route swings from the park around to Tyndall's Point Park where fortifications from the Civil War are still visible. The first shots in four years of intensive fighting in Virginia were fired here on May 3, 1861 when the Union vessel, *USS Yankee*, sailed up the York River. Along the way, you'll learn about the natural history of wetlands and the Chesapeake

When it was built in 1952 to replace ferry traffic at the Point, the George P. Coleman Memorial Bridge, named for a former head of Virginia's tranportation department, was the longest double-swing bridge in the world at 3,750 feet. It is still the longest such bridge in the United States. As traffic loads inched towards triple the bridge's capacity a replacement bridge was built in Norfolk and barged up the York River in 1995. It was carrying traffic only nine days later. This was the first time a bridge of this size had been floated into place, ready to carry traffic.

Bay as well as the military history.

But the main attractions for your dog at Gloucester Point will be the smooth sand beach and swimming in the light waves of the bay. There is also a small grassy area to roll around on after a good swim. For you too.

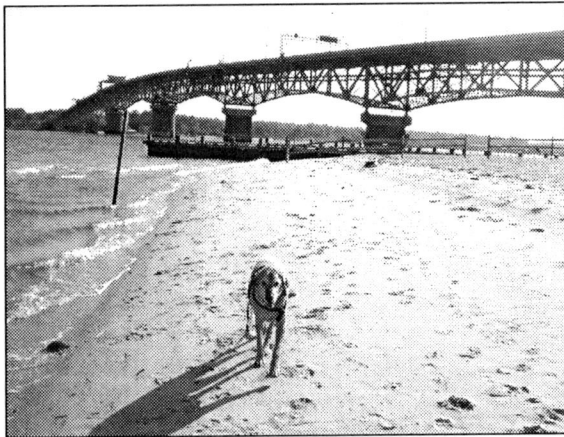

Your dog can admire the Coleman Bridge while playing on the beach at Gloucester Point Beach Park.

Trail Sense: Interpretive signs define the *Point Walk*.

Dog Friendliness
Dogs are welcome in the park and poop bags are provided.
Traffic
Parking is limited in the lot and will fill up during a nice summer day.
Canine Swimming
Excellent dog paddling in the beach area where the water is calmed by a breakwater.
Trail Time
Depends on how much time your dog wants to spend on the beach.

31
Dismal Swamp Canal Trail

The Park

Colonel William Byrd II led a band of surveyors into the swamp in 1728 and the yellow flies, chiggers and ticks he encountered so discouraged him that he described the place as "a vast body of dirt and nastiness." He called it "Dismal" and the name stuck.

George Washington led investors here in 1764 to investigate the building of a canal to extricate timber from the swamp. It wasn't until 1793, however, that slave labor began digging out the waterway between the Elizabeth River in Virginia and the Pasquotank River in North Carolina.

The first flat-bottomed barges went down the 22-mile canal in 1805 and today it is the oldest continually operating canal in the United States. It is recognized as a National Civil Engineering Landmark and is listed on the National Register of Historic Places.

The *Dismal Swamp Canal Trail* opened in July 2005 for hiking, biking, birding and photography.

Chesapeake

Phone Number
- (757) 382-6411

Website
- www.chesapeake.va.us/services/depart/park-rec/dismal_swamp_trail.shtml

Admission Fee
- None

Park Hours
- Daylight hours

Directions
- *Chesapeake*; From I-64 take Exit 292 for Route 190 East (Great Bridge Boulevard). Go right on Route 17 past Route 165 and make a right onto Route 17 Business. Parking for the North Trailhead is 1/2-mile on the left.

The Walks

The *Dismal Swamp Canal Trail* runs into North Carolina; the trail is 8.3 miles long in Virginia. Most canine hikers will be interested in just a chunk, often an out-and-back from the north trailhead. The trail is hard-packed under paw and a roomy ten feet wide, usually with an adequate shoulder. Your dog will be trotting through a leafy forest most of the time along the route.

Trail Sense: A park map is available and the trail sports mile markers every half-mile.

Dog Friendliness
Dogs are allowed to use the *Dismal Swamp Canal Trail*.

Traffic
You will be sharing the trail with bicycles and rollerbladers and horses; no motorized vehicles.

Canine Swimming
The canal area is not developed for swimming access.

Trail Time
Several hours of trail time are available.

32

Rappahannock River Valley NWR

The Park

The Atlantic Flyway Council first proposed a national wildlife refuge on the Rappahannock River in the early 1960s but it did not happen until 1996. Conservationists are aiming at protecting 20,000 acres on the river where birds can find rest and nourishment during migration and a haven in winter. To date the refuge has approached realizing half that total in more than a dozen units along the Rappahannock valley.

The Walks

One of the reasons often given for keeping dogs off trails in National Parks is that dogs disturb wildlife. So you might be surprised to learn about some of the best lands our federal government maintains where you can hike with your dog - our National Wildlife Refuges.

While the priority of National Wildlife Refuges is to manage lands for the benefit of wildlife, human visitors are welcome in 98 percent of the refuges. And most will welcome your dog in as well. And that is the case at Rappahannock River Valley.

What can you expect when you take your dog to a National Wildlife Refuge? The first thing you will notice is that you may have the place to yourself - especially if you come in the off-season. Park managers are not in the business of carving and maintaining hiking trails, however. Like many wildlife refuges some of your best canine hiking will be along lightly-traveled park roads in the main Wilna/Wright Unit.

Northern Neck

Phone Number
- (804) 333-1470

Website
- www.fws.gov/northeast/
rappahannock/

Admission Fee
- None

Park Hours
- Sunrise to sunset

Directions
- *Warsaw*; From US-17, take US-360 E (toward Warsaw) for 4.1 miles. Turn left onto Route 624/Newland Road and go 4.2 miles. Turn left onto Strangeway/Route 636. Follow Strangeway for .2 miles and turn right onto Sandy Lane/Route 640. Follow Sandy Lane for 1.1 miles. Turn left into the refuge.

Your prime destination is the Wilna Pond and a short trail that has been added to the *Virginia Birding and Wildlife Trail*. For a little woodland adventure for your dog check out the trail behind the refuge office that wanders down an old farm road to some actively growing agricultural fields.

Come in the winter to see Virginia's largest population of bald eagles. As many as 395 have been spotted in a single day here.

This mowed trailhead is the exception rather than the rule when it comes to trail maintenance at Rappahannock River Valley NWR.

Trail Sense: There is a map on an information board along the entrance road and that is likely to be your only navigational aid.

Dog Friendliness
Dogs are welcome to hike in the Rappahnnock River Valley refuge.
Traffic
Almost non-existent most of the time.
Canine Swimming
Wilna Pond is for the birds, not the dogs.
Trail Time
About one hour.

33
Deep Creek Lock Park

The Park

The Dismal Swamp Canal is America's oldest continuously operating canal at 202 years and counting. The Deep Creek Lock - near the bridge where Route 17 crosses the canal - was once the location of Mile Marker Zero on the Intracoastal Waterway, 1,087 miles from Miami and 966 from Eastport, Maine.

The village of Deep Creek grew up here when barges carrying lumber from the Dismal Swamp began stopping frequently. By 1850, there were about 50 houses in the village. In 1859 the Albemarle and Chesapeake Canal opened as direct competition for traffic between Elizabeth City and Norfolk.

Chesapeake
Phone Number - None
Website - www.chesapeake.va.us/services/depart/park-rec/deep-creeklockpark.shtml
Admission Fee - None
Park Hours - Sunrise to sunset
Directions - *Chesapeake*; From I-64 take Route 17 Business South. Turn left on Luray Street and follow to the park at the end.

Dismal Swamp Canal wavered on the edge of bankruptcy for many years. Finally, in what might be termed an act of fairness, the government purchased it in 1929.

Today it is managed by the U.S. Army Corps of Engineers and favored by boaters seeking a relaxing, scenic journey as opposed to the faster Albemarle and Chesapeake Route. Folks come to the park to get close-up looks at luxury yachts as the boats wait for the water level to be raised eight feet.

The Walks

This is an odd little park, only 25 acres. The hiking paths are short and unmarked - one route loops through quiet pine-dominated woodlands and the other crosses a small pedestrian bridge onto an island peninsula. This latter path continues as the land on either sand constricts more and more until you can go no more. It is a wild and rooty exploration before you and your dog turn back and head for the more conventional aspects of the park. This can include a game of fetch on a shady grass field - but be careful of the small cemetery from the 1800s in the middle. A lot of character here.

Trail Sense: None.

Dog Friendliness

Dogs are welcome in the park.

Traffic

This is not a typical destination for canine hikers.

Canine Swimming

No swimming around the canal.

Trail Time

Less than an hour.

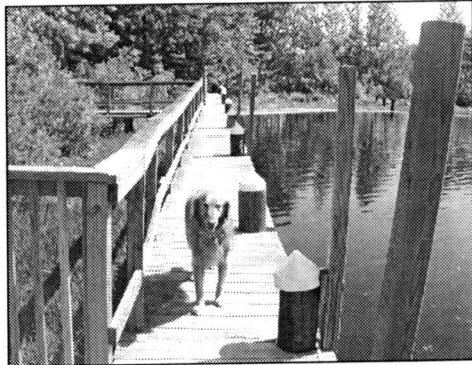

Elizabeth's Dock is a good place for your dog to hang out, watch luxury yachts pass by and dream of sailing to Florida.

83

Camping With Your Dog In The Tidewater

American Heritage RV Park
Williamsburg
On maxton Lane, second left after exiting I-64 at 231A.
open year-round   **(757) 566-2133**

Anvil Campground
Williamsburg
5243 Mooretown Road off Airport Road (Route 645), from I-64 take exit 238 onto Rochambeau Drive (Rte. F-137) and go 1.3 miles to Airport Road.
open year-round   **(757) 565-2300**

Bethpage Camp-Resort
Urbana
Route 602, five miles off US 17.
open April 1 to November 15   **(804) 758-4349**

Cherrystone Family Camping Resort
Cheriton
On Route 680, west of Route 13, 11 miles north of Chesapeake Bay Bridge-Tunnel.
open year-round   **(757) 258-5020**

Chesapeake Bay/Smith Island KOA
Reedville
On Sunnybank Road, two miles from US 360 in Lilian off US 17.
open year-round   **(804) 453-3430**

Chesapeake Campground
Chesapeake
On US 17 (693 S George Washington Highway), 3.5 miles south of I-64, Exit 296.
open year-round   **(757) 485-0149**

Chickahominy Riverfront Park

Williamsburg

At 1350 John Taylor Highway (Route 5), just past junction with Monticello Avenue.

open year-round   **(757) 258-5020**

Chippokes Plantation State Park

Surry

Alliance Road (Route 634), four miles form Route 10.

open year-round   **(757) 294-3625**

First Landing State Park

Virginia Beach

2500 Shore Drive/US 60, 4.5 miles from I-64, Exit 282.

open March 1 to November 30   **(757) 412-2300**

Gosnolds Hope Park

Hampton

901 East Little Back River Road, 2.3 miles north of junction of US 258 via Route 278 and Little Back River Road.

open year-round   **(757) 850-5116**

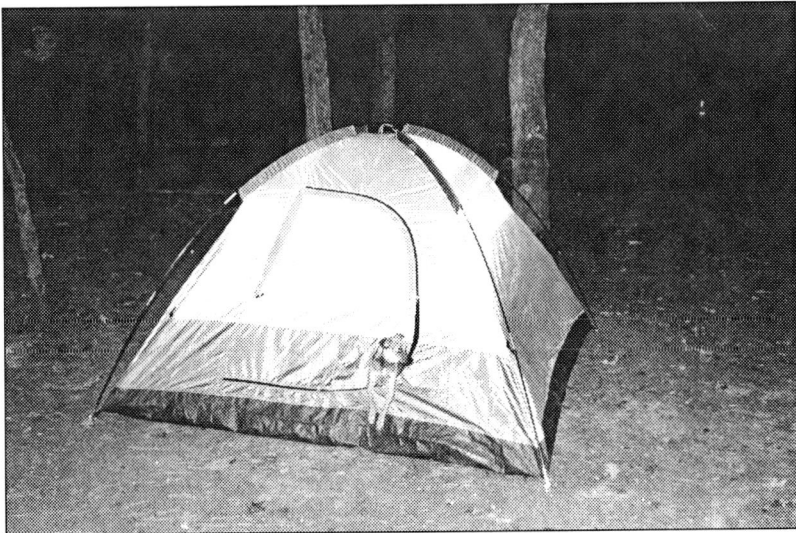

Gloucester Point Family Campground
Hayes
Route 17 to Bray's Point Road, right at fork to Route 656, right onto Low Ground Road, left onto Zack Road, lef ton Campground Road.
open year-round   **(804) 642-4316**

Grey's Point Camp
Topping
At foot of Rappahannock River Bridge on Route 3, 3.25 miles north of US 33.
open April 1 to November 15   **(804) 758-2485**

Heritage Park
Warswaw
2750 Newland Road (Route 324), 2.5 miles off Route 360.
open year-round   **(804) 333-4038**

Holiday Trav-L-Park
Virginia Beach
1075 General Booth Boulevard, 2.5 miles south of I-264 terminus via Pacific Avenue.
open year-round   **(757) 425-5117**

Kiptopeke State Park
Cape Charles
County Road 704 west of Route 13, 2.5 miles north of Chesapeake Bay Bridge-Tunnel.
open March 1 to November 30   **(757) 331-2267**

New Point RV Resort
New Point
On Sand Bank Road (Route 602) off Route 14 East, seven miles past Mathews Court House.
open April 1 to October 31   **(804) 725-5120**

Newport News Park
Newport News
13564 Jefferson Avenue at I-64, Exit 250B.
open year-round   **(757) 888-3333**

North Bay Shore Campground
Virginia Beach
3257 Colechester Road off Sandbridge Road from Princess Anne Road.
open April 15 to October 15 **(757) 426-7911**

North Landing Beach Riverfront Campground
Virginia Beach
161 Princess Anne Road, ten miles from Indian River Road off I-64.
open year-round **(757) 426-6241**

Northwest River Park
Chesapeake
1733 Indian Creek Road, four miles east of Battlefield Boulevard.
open April 1 to November 30 **(757) 421-3145**

Outdoor Resort
Virginia Beach
3665 South Sandpiper Road off Princess Anne Road.
open year-round **(757) 721-2020**

Outdoor World Williamsburg
Williamsburg
I-64 to Exit 231A to Route 607 to route 30 and right at light.
open year-round **(757) 566-3021**

Pine Grove Campground
Chincoteague
5283 Deep Hole Road, north of town off Maddox Boulevard.
open year-round **(757) 336-5200**

Riverside Camp #2 Campground
Lanexa
On Route 627, three miles from Route 60.
open March 1 - November 30 **(804) 966-5536**

Rockahock Campground
Lanexa
Rockahock Road (Route 649) off Route 60, 6.5 miles east of Route 155.
open year-round **(804) 966-8362**

Sandy Bottom Nature Park

Hampton

At the corner of Hampton Roads Center Parkway (West) and Big Bethel Road (Route 600), off I-64, Exit 261A.

open year-round   **(757) 825-4657**

Sunset Beach Resort

Cape Charles

On Route 13, one mile north of Chesapeake Bay Bridge-Tunnel.

open year-round   **(757) 331-4SUN**

Tall Pines Harbor Campground

Temperanceville

On VA 695, six miles west of Route 13, eight miles south of the Maryland/Virginia state line.

open year-round   **(757) 824-0777**

Tom's Cove Park

Chincoteague Island

8128 Beebe Road, east of Main Street 1.5 miles south of town.

open March 1- November 30   **(757) 336-6498**

Virginia Beach KOA

Virginia Beach

1240 General Booth Boulevard, two miles south of I-264 terminus.

open year-round   **(757) 428-1444**

Westmoreland State Park

Montross

On Route 3, east of town.

open year-round   **(804) 493-8821**

Williamsburg KOA

Williamsburg

4000 Newman Road, 1.5 miles from I-64, Exit 234.

open March 1- November 30   **(757) 565-2907**

Your Dog At The Beach

It is hard to imagine many places a dog is happier than at a beach. Whether running around on the sand, jumping in the water or just lying in the sun, every dog deserves a day at the beach. But all too often dog owners stopping at a sandy stretch of beach are met with signs designed to make hearts - human and canine alike - droop: NO DOGS ON BEACH. Below are rules for taking your dog on a day trip to one of our Tidewater beaches.

Chincoteague	No dogs allowed in National Wildlife Refuge
Gloucester Point	Leashed dogs allowed anytime
Hughlett Point	Leashed dogs allowed anytime
Kiptopeke SP	Leashed dogs allowed on the beach
Mathews	No dogs allowed on Bethel Beach
Virginia Beach Back Bay NWR	Dogs allowed October 1 to March 31
False Cape SP	Dogs allowed by boat or Beach Trail Nov-Mar; by boat only Apr to Sept and not in swimming areas
First Landing SP	Dogs allowed on beach
Little Island Park	Dogs allowed on beach but not in swimming areas
North End (41st to 80tth St)	Dogs allowed on beach the day after Labor Day to the Friday before Memorial Day; in summer dogs allowed on residential beaches above 42nd Street before 10 am and after 6 pm
The Strip (1st to 40th St)	Dogs allowed on beach the day after Labor Day to the Friday before Memorial Day

Tips For Taking Your Dog To The Beach

- The majority of dogs can swim and love it, but dogs entering the water for the first time should be tested; never throw a dog into the water. Start in shallow water and call your dog's name - or try to coax him in with a treat or toy. Always keep your dog within reach.

- Another way to introduce your dog to the water is with a dog that already swims and is friendly with your dog. Let your dog follow his friend.

- If your dog begins to doggie paddle with his front legs only, lift his hind legs and help him float. He should quickly catch on and will keep his back end up.

- Swimming is a great form of exercise, but don't let your dog overdo it. He will be using new muscles and may tire quickly.

- Be careful of strong tides that are hazardous for even the best swimmers.

- Cool ocean water is tempting to your dog. Do not allow him to drink too much sea water. Salt in the water will make him sick. Salt and other minerals found in the ocean can damage your dog's coat so regular bathing is essential.

- Check with a lifeguard for daily water conditions - dogs are easy targets for jellyfish and sea lice.

- Dogs can get sunburned, especially short-haired dogs and ones with pink skin and white hair. Limit your dog's exposure when the sun is strong and apply sunblock to his ears and nose 30 minutes before going outside.

- If your dog is out of shape, don't encourage him to run on the sand, which is strenuous exercise and a dog that is out of shape can easily pull a tendon or ligament.

Index To Parks

Printed in the United States
125629LV00004B/13/A

9 780979 707407